To Marjorie
From Brian

Best wishes
Bin.

Mara!

Africa bridges the gap between Church and Life

Bill Jones

With a foreword by
The Rt Revd Hilkiah Omindo Deya
Bishop of Mara

ALIQUID NOVUM

Published by

Aliquid Novum

aliquidnovum@btinternet.com

© Bill Jones 2013

ISBN 978-0-9926806-0-2

All Rights Reserved

No part of this book may be reproduced in any form,
by photocopying or by any electronic or mechanical means,
including information storage or retrieval systems,
without permission in writing from both the copyright
owner and the publisher of this book.

Printed and bound in the UK
by Inky Little Fingers
Churcham, Gloucester, GL2 8AX.

For the most tolerant of wives

"Do you realise that you are God's partner? When there is someone hungry, God wants to perform the miracle of feeding that person. But it won't any longer be through manna falling from heaven. Normally, more usually, God can do nothing until we provide God with the means, the bread and the fish, to feed the hungry."

Desmond Tutu
God has a dream

Contents

	Foreword	11
1	Introduction	13
2	What's it like in Mara?	20
3	Pushing the week	28
4	Discipleship & Mission	40
5	God is not a stranger	55
6	The ABC of AIDS	62
7	Dangerous wildlife	74
8	Money, money, money	87
9	Taking charge	102
10	The Key to Life	108
	• *Issenye Nursery School*	109
	• *ACT Mara Primary School*	110
	• *Issenye High School*	115
	• *Mara Vocational Training Centre*	126
	• *Bunda Girls' School*	129
11	The generation game	132
12	Buhemba	137
13	Offshoots	147
14	Mogabiri	156
15	All that glisters	163
16	Water for Life	173
17	Healthy living	181
18	Finale	191
	Postscript	200

Equator
Tanzania

Mara Region's 3 Dioceses

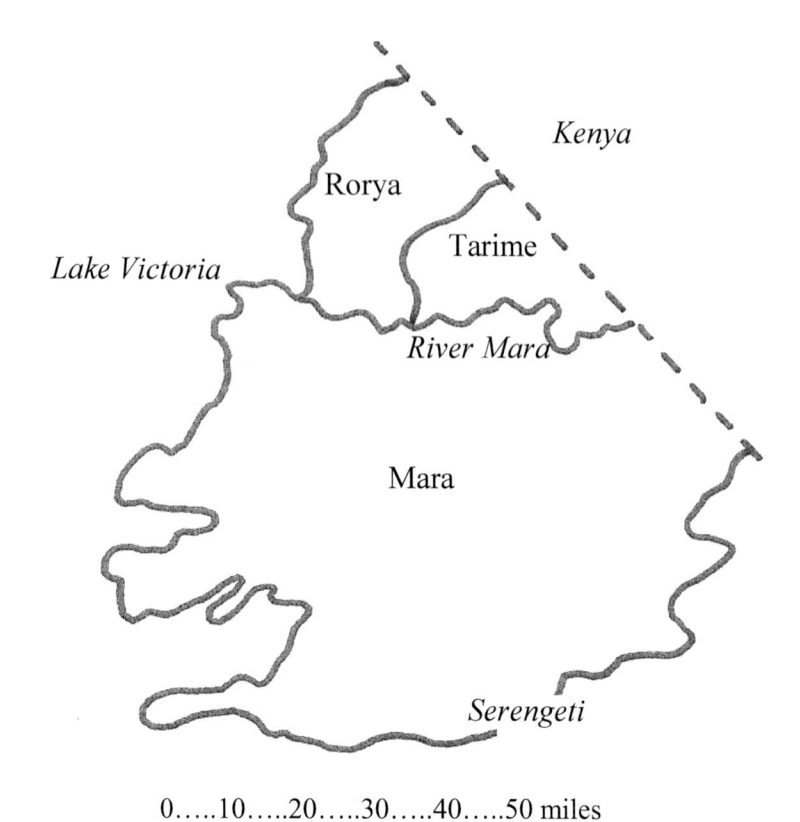

Kenya

Rorya

Tarime

Lake Victoria

River Mara

Mara

Serengeti

0…..10…..20…..30…..40…..50 miles

Foreword

Nobody is better qualified than Bill Jones to write this comprehensive account of the Church's work here in Mara Region. From the earliest days of our link with Wakefield Diocese, Bill has been a constant supporter of, and active participant in, the growth and development of Christian witness here in Africa, and especially in Mara.

From 1989 to 1996 Bill lived in Issenye, a distant village in the Serengeti where, together with his wife Maureen, he founded our diocesan secondary school and health centre. Issenye has continued to flourish and is now always close to the top of our national league tables. Issenye educates more than 500 young men and women every year in a strong Christian environment and many of its former pupils are now in positions of authority throughout Tanzania. Bill and Maureen built a strong educational foundation for Issenye Secondary School.

Bill then took over as Mara Link Officer, based in Wakefield, and established many of the core principles that underpin our relationship. He has escorted many groups of visitors to and from Mara and there is barely a corner of our diocese that he has not penetrated. Bill was made Lay Canon of the Diocese of Mara as a result of his dedication to the ministry of the Church in the Diocese of Mara and his good advice to the Bishop of Mara.

The link with Wakefield has grown over the years and is now so strong that we feel to be one diocese, living out the reality of what we say each Sunday:

> "Though we are many we are one body
> because we share in the one bread."

That bread is the body of Christ and we in Mara, along with our brothers and sisters in Wakefield, strive with all our hearts and minds to do Christ's work as his body here on earth. Doing it *'bega kwa bega'* (or 'shoulder to shoulder') brings us together in ways that afford much happiness to all who take part in this Great Commission.

I warmly welcome this book which has been carefully researched here on the ground from Bill's own experiences in Mara rather than from a distance, and I have no hesitation in recommending it to readers in Wakefield and beyond. It gives a full picture of how we in Mara try to reach out holistically to our communities and deliver the Gospel message of 'abundant life'.

I also hope it may encourage you to visit us!

Bwana Asifiwe! (Praise the Lord!)

+Hilkiah Omindo Deya
Bishop of Mara

Chapter 1
Introduction

The Diocese of Mara was born in 1985. A diocese, the name the Church gives to a collection of parishes in a given geographical area, comes to life when it is carved out of an existing one in order to make it more manageable. At least, that is what people say, but perhaps the expression relates to 'calving' rather than carving, and the analogy is with that of an iceberg splitting into smaller sections as the result of internal pressures. The part that breaks off rolls unsteadily into the sea and sways from side to side until it finds its centre of gravity and assumes an upright position. What happened in Mara was that the Diocese of Victoria Nyanza, in Tanzania, became too large to be managed from its administrative centre, Mwanza. And so the northern section, up towards Kenya and centred on the River Mara, was cast loose as the newly created Diocese of Mara with its administrative centre at Musoma, on the shores of Lake Victoria. Abruptly, parishes which had felt to be far from the seat of power became proud of their new status under the guidance of their own leader, Gershom Nyaronga.

The newly created Bishop Gershom was no stranger to Mara, being a native of Buganjo, one of its twelve parishes. He was given scant resources to manage his new diocese and often talked of the two hundred thousand shillings with which he had to start up – about £350 at that time. Gershom's strength was his gift for evangelism, and he set about his new job with gusto, travelling round his diocese to deliver fiery sermons and enthuse people with his love of the Gospel and his desire for development. He also began to look for friends.

In that same year of 1985, another newly promoted bishop began his ministry in faraway West Yorkshire. David Hope, (later Bishop of London and then Archbishop of York) inherited a very different set-up. Wakefield Diocese had been created almost a hundred years before and was well established in its Yorkshire setting. One of the new bishop's first decisions was to set up a link with a diocese in a developing country. Writing later, he said:

"As a fairly new Bishop of Wakefield I was invited to participate in a 'Partners in World Mission' consultation with the Anglican Church in Tanzania. I met Gershom Nyaronga, who told me he had become Bishop of the new Diocese of Mara, and that he was having to start from scratch. I suggested the possibility of a link with Wakefield and he responded positively."

The two newly appointed bishops steered their respective dioceses into a friendship that lasts to this day and that is the envy of many, both in Britain and in Africa. The relationship is seen as strong and enduring and it is inconceivable that any future bishop of either diocese would consider dissolving it.

Twenty years later, each diocese found itself at a crossroads, but of different kinds. Wakefield was facing the prospect of a merger with neighbouring Leeds/Ripon and Bradford dioceses, whilst Mara was engaged in splitting into three. At the time of writing, the crucial decision to merge Wakefield with its neighbours has just been made, but in Mara, the new 'calving' process happened three years ago. The administrative area of Tanzania known as Mara Region, located to the south of Kenya and north of the Serengeti Plain, now contains 'New Mara' in the south, with Rorya and Tarime in the north, beyond the River Mara itself. (See map, Page 8). Bishop Hilkiah remains in 'New Mara', Bishop John Adiema is in Rorya and Bishop Mwita Akiri is in Tarime.

The drive for this division has been the hectic speed of church growth in Mara. Despite the vast distances, transport difficulties, lack of roads and poor communications, the original 12 parishes had grown to an astonishing 132 by 2010 and Hilkiah felt that he was no longer able to maintain the close contact with his clergy that he deemed essential for his style of leadership. Rather than revel in the increased power and prestige of an enlarged 'empire' he chose to encourage the northern parts of the diocese to split off and continue the process of growth.

For those of us living in a society where the Church is increasingly marginalised and congregations are shrinking, it is wonderfully uplifting to be linked with one where the opposite is happening, but it is also baffling. After all, we adhere to the same faith, so why is it working so well in Africa but visibly struggling here? What is the secret, we are bound to ask? Are there things we can learn?

One thing which strikes all visitors to Mara is the extent to which the Church reaches into the everyday lives of people there – whether or not they are Christians.

Its very practical social projects offer 'pies today' to paraphrase Desmond Tutu, Archbishop Emeritus, Nobel prize winner, former chairman of South Africa's Truth and Reconciliation Commission, and international treasure, whose influence extends far beyond the Anglican Church he serves. In his 2004 book, God has a Dream, Tutu says the following:

"The religion I believe in is not what Marx castigated as the opiate of the people. A Church that tries to pacify us, telling us not to concentrate on the things of this world but of the other, the next world, needs to be treated with withering scorn and contempt as being not only irrelevant but actually blasphemous. It deals with pie in the sky when you die – and I am not interested, nobody is interested, in post mortem pies. People around the world want their pies here and now."

Despite its army of selfless clergy and willing volunteers who offer untold hours of service to the community, the Church in Britain too often manages to give the appearance of turning its back on the world of today. It is difficult to avoid the conclusion that, for many people, an ever widening gap exists between Church and ordinary life.

This impression is not helped by our apparent obsession with bitter and self-harming arguments about gender and sexual orientation. They have taken the place of discussions about how many angels can balance on the end of a pin. At other times we allow ourselves to be seen as offering nothing but Archbishop Tutu's 'post mortem pies' to compensate for a less than satisfactory time spent in the here and now.

This book will look, then, at the startling growth of a very different Church in one specific area of Africa, but which is mirrored in many other parts of that continent. In particular, it will explore the ways in which the Church in Mara delivers 'pies today' or the abundant life promised in John 10:10 to which Bishop Hilkiah refers in his foreword. We will skip the 'churchy' side of church. Readers may take it for granted that clergy are trained, hymns are sung, God is worshipped and that evangelism is ardently pursued. This account begins at the point where, at the end of the Anglican liturgy, we say 'send us *out* in the power of your spirit, to *live* and *work* to your praise and glory'. In other words, we spend our time in church preparing for life outside – which is where the real work of being a Christian begins.

Ask anyone in the hierarchy of all three of Mara's dioceses what its priorities are, and the answer is invariably evangelism. But the way in which that is carried out is not, I believe, what is generally understood by the term in Britain. From its grassroots help with agricultural development, through its vocational training courses, primary and secondary education centres to its rural health centre on the edge of the Serengeti, and tireless work to reduce the effects of AIDS and malaria, the Church in Mara is responding to the real, daily needs of people, regardless of religious or tribal affiliation. Its approach calls to mind the words attributed to St Francis of Assisi; 'Preach the Gospel always – use words if necessary.' And very often, words take second place.

This vigorous and Gospel-driven determination to preach the Good News through service, and this phenomenal rate of growth - a new parish opening every eleven weeks on average - cannot help but fascinate churchgoers in Britain more accustomed to hear of parishes shrinking and merging than growing and splitting. Listening to people whose lives are being transformed by the practical ways in which the Church in Mara works inspires a conviction that we must listen to those whom we are more accustomed to teach.

Africa, of course, is Africa – and Britain is Britain. The days when the Church of England was the main provider of educational, social and health services in Britain are over, and it is right that the state should have assumed responsibility for them. If that leaves the Church floundering without an identified role in society it is up to its leaders and its members to identify new ways of serving the community. After all, it is clear that our welfare state does not meet all the needs of all the people, and that there are many gaps through which people can fall. Many individual churches and the Church as an institution make strenuous efforts to fill such gaps, or engage in advocacy to persuade the state to do so. But often we fail to do either and assume that 'they' will, or should, do something about it.

The pages that follow will look at how African Christians working in extraordinarily difficult circumstances find ways of not only filling the gaps, but also of filling their pews. With churches in Africa growing faster even than those in Britain are shrinking, have they found the way to bridge the gap between Church and life? Have we been, perhaps, too busy thinking about how we can help Africa to consider how Africa can help us?

This description of the Church at work in Mara stops short of suggesting what that help might be. My aim here is to show what the Church in Mara is doing, especially in its outreach to people, along with the suggestion that we might be able to consider it as a template for a new understanding of what 'mission' might mean for Britain in the 21st Century. I have also tried to convey what it is like actually to be in Mara, and I gladly echo Bishop Hilkiah's open invitation to embark on a *safari* that will be a life-changing experience.

My own association with Tanzania began in 1982 and with Mara in 1989. The words that follow are a personal view, and therefore subjective. They are the result of ten years working in Tanzania and numerous return visits, including nine weeks in 2013 spent principally in 'New Mara', from where most of the following examples of the Church's work are taken.

I thank everyone who has helped me try to understand the work of the Church in Africa, especially the project workers and clients who tolerated my intrusive presence so gracefully. I owe a special word of thanks to Canon Arthur Mauya, Mara's Director of Education and Wakefield Link Officer, for his tireless attention to my needs and for his much valued friendship. I am also indebted to Mike Jones and Roy Clements for helping me to see wood amongst the trees.

I apologise in advance for those shortcomings, errors or misunderstandings where the whole picture may have been lost in translation.

Bill Jones, June 2013

Chapter 2
What's it like in Mara?

This is the question most frequently asked of visitors returning from there. Mara Region, with which the original Diocese of Mara exactly coincided, sits in the north western corner of Tanzania, wedged between neighbouring Kenya to the north, Lake Victoria to the west, and the mighty Serengeti plain to the south and east. It covers approximately 30,000 square km, which makes it fifteen times the size of West Yorkshire, although almost a quarter of that is in Lake Victoria and another quarter is in the Serengeti National Park. That still leaves a sizeable land area, with the majority of communities linked only by mud roads subject to seasonal variation. Most have no services such as electricity, piped water, sewage disposal or public transport.

Mobile telephones have dramatically transformed communications in recent years, and as wireless technology takes hold, internet access will make even bigger changes in people's lives. For most, however, life is a struggle, with each family within one failed harvest of disaster. Most people are not in paid jobs and so, in our terms, are unemployed. But this belies the reality of their lives which are full of work. At its most basic level, people in Mara grow food and eat it. When the rains come in the right quantity and at the right time, there is enough to eat and a little over.

When they are not planting, weeding, irrigating, or harvesting their maize, sweet potatoes, millet, cassava, onions, bananas, pawpaws and mangoes they are collecting water and fuel for cooking, repairing or building their houses, or tending their livestock. When the rains fail, laboriously planted seeds fail to germinate and are devoured by insects. Food becomes scarce and children arc put to bed hungry. There are no food banks.

Even those Tanzanians fortunate enough to have paid work are expected to grow food. The late and great founding president Julius Nyerere could regularly be seen tending his *shamba* at Butiama, in the heart of Mara. Salaries have to go a long way round extended families and there is a strong expectation that those with money, the minority, will help those who are without, the majority. Young people who are helped with their education and who make it into the world of salaries then give a helping hand to their younger siblings and so a virtuous circle is set up. The national policy of self-reliance asserts itself without recourse to government grants, student loans, housing benefit or subsidies.

Indeed, the government could not afford such extravagances even were it so minded. Health care, street lighting, tarmac roads, pensions, housing benefit, child allowances, garbage collection, social services, piped water, mains drainage, electricity – all the things we take for granted in Britain – are paid for out of taxation. In Britain one has to be very poor or very rich to avoid taxation, and despite the ingenious practices to which wealthy people resort, most of us have it removed from our pay packets before we even see it, let alone are tempted to spend it. But subsistence farms yield little tax revenue. Even when money changes hands at the weekly market, it would be difficult for Tanzania's Inland Revenue to keep track of cow or chicken, and it is easy for each party to keep things informal.

At its best, the traditional life of a villager in Mara is idyllic. The extended family unit works co-operatively, with each of its members playing a useful part in its continuing success. Even the youngest toddler, newly released from his mother's back to make room for the next in line, totters after his father as he plants maize seeds when the rains have set in, treading them into the soft earth with his bare feet and learning what it is to be a man. His sister practises carrying stones on her head, starting with pebbles, then gradually building up until she can balance larger and heavier objects with apparent ease, until the day arrives when a 20 litre bucket presents no problem.

Older boys and girls help in the daily search for *kuni*, or fuel wood, for cooking. Even the oldest grandmother, crippled with the infirmity of age, sits cross-legged under the overhanging thatch of her hut shelling beans for the shared evening meal. Each family member is valued for what they are and for what they can do, in contrast to the reality of more developed societies where only the economically active age band is perceived as 'having a job'.

The land provides for all the family's needs. If a new house is needed as the family grows, there is no building society to go to for a mortgage. The family and its friends gather stout timbers for the uprights, sinking them into the earth in a perfect circle. Whippy branches are then laced around them, and straight but light weight sisal poles lashed together to make a conical roof. Grasses are gathered to make thatch, then stones are pushed into the gaps in the walls and the whole edifice is caked in mud to make a smooth finish. The entire process takes two or three days and costs nothing.

Maintenance? Well, a bit of grass may blow off – it is easily replaced. In severe rainy conditions, a section of wall may wash away. But the mud doesn't travel very far, and it is easily scooped back into place. When the house is no longer needed, it quickly decays and slips unobtrusively back into the landscape from which it was formed. There is no discernible environmental impact.

As for food, there are no supermarkets in the villages. Each family grows and rears most of what it eats. Everyone has a few hens which provide eggs and meat. Most have a goat or two, and many aspire to have a cow. Everyone grows something to eat. Maize, millet, cassava and sweet potatoes are the mainstays of the diet. Maize is used to make a porridge-like mixture which comes either thin (*uji*) or thick (*ugali*). *Uji* may be sweetened with sugar if available, or even mixed with milk instead of water. *Ugali* may be enriched with a small amount of meat or gravy, perhaps with onions or tomatoes added according to season. Those close to a river or to Lake Victoria may catch fish.

Of course, not everything a family needs can be grown. Medicines, cooking oil, paraffin for lighting, clothing, school books, a mattress, radio or bicycle have to be bought, and the cash comes from surplus crops if the harvest is good. If it fails, those things have to wait. The sale of a cow is the failsafe way of raising money quickly, but that is a step to be pondered deeply as cows are wealth and are accumulated like walking bank deposits against a rainy day.

Like all idylls, this 'Good Life' picture of subsistence living is often illusory. A rainy day in Mara is actually a good day, as it means that seeds planted will germinate and crops will grow. But it doesn't always rain. And when that happens, disaster follows. Food becomes scarce and whole families go hungry. Growing evidence of climate change has made weather patterns increasingly unpredictable, and even without that there is always the hungry time, when the fruits of one harvest are exhausted before the next crop ripens. But if the next crop fails to materialise, despair sets in. Not only is there less food in the affected area, but what little is there shoots up in price in response to pressures of supply and demand. Shortage of food leads to malnutrition, which reduces resistance to disease and, because there is no money to pay for medicines or hospital care, illnesses remain untreated and the good life turns sour.

So how does the Church, an institution introduced from Europe, serve such a very different community than the one from which it sprang? With little or no back-up from the state, no wealthy Church Commissioners to fund its bishops and no centuries of endowments to cushion it from economic reality, it is unsurprising to learn that the Church in Africa vigorously pursues any possible source of support from its comparatively comfortable friends in the west. Mara was fortunate that, in its infancy, it attracted the support of a diocese dedicated to mission in the shape of Wakefield. David Hope put all his considerable weight behind making the relationship work and his successors, Nigel McCulloch and Stephen Platten, have maintained and accelerated the momentum he began.

There have been frequent visits, in each direction, and these have made the Mara Link real, both in the eyes of those fortunate enough to make the trip and in the hearts of those offering friendship and hospitality in West Yorkshire and in Mara. Wakefield is far from being a wealthy diocese and yet the generosity of its parishioners has astonished many of its more prosperous neighbours. Time after time they have responded to crises of which they have been made aware – whether caused by drought, disease, death or simple poverty. On an everyday basis, year by year, they have funded the building of churches, classrooms, laboratories, a rural health centre, water harvesting schemes, health campaigns and a bible school. They have paid the school fees of hundreds of young people. They have sent typewriters, computers, duplicators, blankets, bandages, medical and scientific equipment, mosquito nets, bicycles, exercise and text books, ball point pens, clothing, shoes, generators and calculators.

One result of such generosity has been, in Mara, the conviction among some parishioners that Wakefield is an endless source of money; and in Wakefield, that the purpose of the link is to funnel our comparative wealth into the pockets of our less fortunate partners in Africa. Such thinking is denied at both ends of the link, and the concept of progress *'bega kwa bega'* (shoulder to shoulder) is the preferred image. We want to lean on each other, and to learn from each other.

The problem with that has been the difficulty that Wakefield experiences in accepting that Mara has much to offer. It is often asserted that we can learn from their spirituality and whilst that is so, the myth that we are the practical ones and they the spiritual ones in the partnership is unfair to both. It relies on a stereotypical view of the spirit filled African, poor but happy with his simple life, and the money-grubbing European, weighed down with worldly goods but dried up inside and bereft of an inner life.

I have been asked in Mara 'What can we give to our friends in Wakefield' and it has been difficult to answer. Bishop Hilkiah once suggested having a collection throughout the diocese for some project in Wakefield. The idea was met with a stunned silence when I relayed it home. "What is the point of us sending money to them and then getting some of it back?" I was asked. Does this reaction hint at a reluctance to treat our partners as equals? Any such collection made in Mara would, of course, be modest, but the biblical story of the widow's mite makes it clear that the worth of a gift should be measured by the ability of the donor to give rather than by its intrinsic monetary value.

But if we are unable to accept money, I hope that the following cameos of life in Mara may suggest other gifts which we should be ready to grasp with both hands.

The wheel has yet to reach all parts of Mara

But when it arrives, it is well used

Chapter 3
Pushing the week

The tour I was offered of the Mara diocesan headquarters in Musoma didn't take long. We passed the labelled offices of Integrated Community Development, Christian Education, Health, the Evangelism & Mission, Empowerment of Women, Malaria and Hygiene, AIDS-ABC, Mothers Union and so on, but every door was firmly locked.

"Where are they all?" I asked the ever helpful Arthur Mauya, Diocesan Director of Education and Wakefield Link Officer.

"They are at work," he said, with a smile. "You'll find them in their offices on Monday morning, but then they get on with their jobs." Obviously work in Mara means getting out of the office. Next day, I got out with them.

The cyclist wobbled towards us with an improbable number of bananas balanced on his carrier causing him to strain every perspiring muscle on the least of adverse gradients. A youth dressed in tattered clothing drew alongside him, pushing a barrow piled high with Nile Perch, the fierce predator which threatens to wipe out all other species in the adjacent Lake Victoria, but which is itself in danger of being fished out of existence by the greatest predator of them all – man. Both were making their way to Musoma's market where they hoped to sell their produce.

We cleared the town and headed south, parallel to the lake shore on our right, but rarely seeing it, and with the broad Mara River estuary on our left. We were heading for Bunda. The crowds thinned out and we accelerated, then slowed down again to negotiate broken sections of asphalt waiting for repair. One stretch of the road had been stripped of old tarmac in readiness for a new topping, and we now bumped carefully round massive concrete bridges being constructed to span the many water courses that drain the Serengeti into the lake. It is rumoured that the Chinese contractors making the bridges include snakes in their diet. They live in their own large camp and are not seen in town.

An hour of steady progress passed, then we left the road to follow a mud track which became increasingly narrow. We moved at a crawl, crushing the vegetation on either side and releasing fragrant clouds of mint into the air. The path became ever more difficult to negotiate until Laddi, our driver, said that this was as far as he could take us. He stayed with the car to protect it. We climbed out and walked. The ground was uneven, dry and sandy.

I was with Sikunjema from Mara's Integrated Community Development Programme, ICDP. Her name means 'Good Day.' She introduced me to Farida, a young Muslim woman she described as a 'farm motivator' who had been waiting for us and who now joined us on our walk. Farida is employed by the government to encourage groups to start their own agricultural projects.

The two young women were clearly well acquainted and they compared notes as we walked.

By now the sun was high in the sky and searingly hot. Both women easily outpaced me, but obligingly adjusted their speed to mine when they saw me struggling over the uneven ground. Multi-coloured lizards did spasmodic press-ups on the rocks as we approached, then hurled themselves off into the undergrowth when we got close. Seeds popped out of their pods as the day's gathering heat burst their cases. We rounded a bend and were greeted by a group of eight women who readily laid down their hoes as we reached them.

They were tilling a patch of land close to a sluggish stream from which a young boy fetched bucket after bucket of water which he splashed carefully over the soil. They were members of a small co-operative and were sowing a second crop of *sukuma-wiki* (push-the week), a spinach-like plant so called because it grows easily and quickly, enabling a family to reach the end of the week free of hunger. Next to it was a patch of carrots, almost ready for harvesting, and salad crops, bright green against the recently watered ground.

Sikunjema has been working with this group for a year with the aim of giving its members, all women, food on the table, and an income from the sale of their produce. The initial seeds came from the diocese and Sikunjema makes fortnightly visits to ensure that the contract agreed between them is being fulfilled. This means maintaining a work schedule, following good practice and keeping proper accounts. Almost as importantly as the food and the income it provides, this project is giving them the confidence to be more assertive in their relationship with their husbands and with society in general in this still patriarchal part of the world.

We moved on to the next part of the village, still on foot and I was feeling the heat. I donned my hat and took a drink out of the water bottle that was sharing the rucksack with my camera. After a while we came to a group of men resting in the shade of a glossy-leaved mango tree and we sank gratefully into the chairs vacated for us. This group had embarked on a more ambitious project in which they were switching from traditional local cattle – the ubiquitous hump-backed *zebu* that originated in India – to an improved strain of dairy cows produced by selective cross-breeding that combines the quality of European breeds with the hardiness of the local strain. The advantage of such cows is that they produce ten times the amount of milk, so the attraction is obvious. To achieve such an output, however, the farmers have to learn new ways of looking after their animals. It's called zero-grazing.

Instead of letting them range over a vast area of land, as their forefathers did for centuries, they now build a stockade and a shelter in which to house them, and they bring their food to them – having first grown it. It sounds like a good deal for the cows - hotel living with all their needs supplied and little to do all day but wait for the next meal. The structure the farmers had built looked ramshackle, but sturdy enough and sufficiently low-tech to be copied easily by friends and neighbours. I asked one of the men where they obtained their first cow.

"It was a gift from the church," he said. "First they taught us this new way of keeping cattle, and how to build the *kibanda*, then they gave us one of these modern cows, and it was already pregnant. When its calf was born we had to give it back so that they could pass it on to another group, but after that we could keep them for ourselves. Now we have our own bull and we are able to give calves to other farmers as well."

We moved on yet again - another exhausting walk to a small house with a satellite dish standing incongruously beside it. There is no electricity in this remotest of spots, but somehow they are plugged into the world. A mixed group of men and women greeted us warmly. They were sawing planks of wood to make the floor of a new goat house which they had constructed from sticks and mud, but with a bright silver corrugated iron roof sparkling in the sun. They were being supervised by Benson, the government's District Agricultural Extension Officer. It was clear that he, too, has a good working relationship with Sikunjema.

As with the cows, the objective is to raise an improved breed of animals which, if appropriately housed and fed, will produce milk for consumption and for sale. The very idea of keeping goats for their milk is novel in Mara, where they have traditionally been kept only for their meat. To understand the reluctance to accept such a concept we would have to consider how we feel about the idea of drinking horse's milk, as they do across the steppes of Asia.

"How did you persuade them?" I asked Benson.

"We conducted a blind tasting," he grinned. "And nobody could tell the difference. After that, it was quite easy." We were privileged to see the first goats introduced to their new home. They peered out at us through the slats of their unfamiliar surroundings, then devoured with gusto the fresh elephant grass brought to them from the nearby plot where the farmers had grown it. Zero grazing in action.

This revolution in farming methods is gradually taking hold, and the Church's role is crucial. By co-operating with local government officials in the planning and execution of projects like this, and by injecting a modest amount of capital for animals, seeds, corrugated iron and other materials, the Church has established strong credibility as an institution that is 'here to help'.

We left them and walked on to find another group with a different approach to development, but once again in collaboration with the Church. They had set up a seed bed nursery where they were producing new varieties of sweet potato which are more nutritious than the standard variety and also more resistant to disease. We were joined by Shabani, another government agricultural officer. He showed me the tubers, and cut one open to reveal that inside they are orange coloured - more like a carrot than a potato.

"People don't like the colour at first," he told me, "but when we teach them that they have more vitamins and that they will resist the diseases that have affected their crops for the last few years, they soon change their minds!"

Further down the hill, we were taken to a large, square pond, clearly artificial. It was their fish farm, where they are raising tilapia – the tastiest of fish. Standing in the water but close to the edge was a rickety structure whose purpose defeated me.

"That is where we keep our rabbits," I was told.

"But why is it standing in the water?" I asked. They pointed to the fish moving around underneath the sturdy hutch. "All the rabbit droppings fall through the floor," Shabani said, "and there is still enough nutrient in them to provide food for the fish. It is a symbiotic relationship." Close to the fish farm there was a sturdy pump with a newly made cement base and shiny metal handle.

"This well was not functioning properly," Shabani said, "but the Anglican Church came and dug it out before fixing this cover and new pump mechanism. Now, you can see that there is no contamination, so the people get clean water and reduce the risk of contracting water-borne diseases." The fish farm, the rabbits and the pump were all the result of church intervention and were all contributing to an improved life style for the people of this village.

Next day, Sikunjema took me to meet a group of men and women the Church is helping in a remarkably different way. Together, they have set up 'Vicoba,' which stands for Village Community Bank and is a form of credit union into which all the members make regular contributions which earn them shares in the bank. The setup is formal, with a chairman, secretary and treasurer. I asked the treasurer what she does with the money and she told me it goes straight into the regular bank at nearby Bunda town. I asked what amounts are borrowed and she said they vary according to the needs and the credit rating of the borrower. This is affected by prompt repayment, usually within three months to a year, and by the number of shares held. Loans have been used for a variety of needs over the three year history of the village bank, ranging from a new bed to a year's school fees. In value they have ranged between £40 and £800 and members are quick to tell me that they have been life-savers for many families.

The Church's input has been to instruct, supervise, and encourage the group, and to inject a small amount of capital to get things going. Towards the end of our meeting I invited them to put any questions they might have. They asked for my advice about how to improve their lives, but I was so lost in admiration for how they are already going about it that I could only offer lame congratulations on what they have achieved. As we left, I spotted the hand painted sign outside their tiny office. It declared that it belongs to the '*Kikundi Cha Tujipe Moyo*' - 'Self Encouragement Group'.

The wording is significant, implying that the group's members feel ownership of the enterprise, and this principle of enablement by the Church, of encouraging people to believe that they have the resources to help themselves, is built into many of Mara's diocesan projects. The approach is always consultative and participatory, with target communities given full rein to express their hopes and fears, and other agencies, government or otherwise, consulted and co-operated with at every opportunity.

In all the encounters detailed above, I saw no attempt to evangelise or recruit into the Anglican Church. The talk was all about food crops, cattle, fish, rabbits, goats, small loans, water, pest control, nutrition, health, gender issues, record keeping and development. Some of the people declared themselves to be 'pagan' whilst others came from different Christian denominations including Pentecostal and Seventh Day Adventist groups. All agreed that the Church was 'a good thing'. And, of course, they are bound to ask themselves 'Why do these people do this?' The answer to that question is simply that they can do no other. The commitment to a gospel-driven life of unconditional service to the community is built into the diocesan mission statement: *'To be the best Christian provider of spiritual and development services in Mara Region'*

Back at diocesan headquarters I asked about the spiritual element and was told that the ICDP workers are like John the Baptist, preparing a way in the wilderness for the Word which will follow. And clients who have benefited from the programme often implore the diocese to open a parish in their area. It's how the Church grows.

Community development through the ICDP is what Bishop Hilkiah calls his 'first child' and it is dear to his heart. As a new bishop he inherited two major projects (Buhemba and Mogabiri), both inspirational in their own ways, but whose effect was limited to the geographical locations in which they were set. His vision was to create something which could be taken into every corner of the diocese 'like Panadol', he said, which would address the needs of the people where they are. He smiled as he recalled that he thought he knew what those needs were, but that when he initiated a survey to actually ask people what they wanted, he discovered that their priorities did not coincide with his. An early lesson – don't tell people what they need, ask them!

Since 2001 ICDP has interacted with more than 10,000 beneficiaries in 32 villages. It has improved crop and livestock production, introduced fish farming and bee keeping, protected and improved natural water sources, built water tanks to enable rain water harvesting, and contributed to the building of classrooms and teachers' houses. Importantly, alongside each of these activities it has also provided training and encouragement for self-motivated groups of villagers to manage their affairs more effectively and release the talents and resources within their own communities. The target for 2017 is for ICDP to be active in 80 villages.

Reading the project's various write-ups is inspirational. There is talk of 'transforming lives through the power of the Gospel', 'sustainable social and economic development from locally available resources', 'responsibility and accountability', 'acknowledging the potential of the individual', and many more pointers to the ethical starting point of everything the ICDP does.

When it comes to the activities themselves they are, quite literally in many cases, rooted in the earth rather than an aspirational wish list. *'Training farmers in improved horticultural production', 'promotion of cross breeding local cattle with improved milk-yielding strains', 'establishing demonstration plots', 'training in the establishment of fish farms', 'introduction of energy saving stoves', 'awareness training on nutritional issues', 'demonstration of rainwater harvesting techniques', 'starter capital for small-scale projects'*......the list goes on, and every element is down to earth, practical, relevant to the daily lives of villagers in an impoverished rural community, and geared to the improvement of their circumstances.

Apart from the initial statement that lives are to be transformed through the power of the Gospel there is no attempt to bang on about religion – it is taken for granted that the Church is vitally interested in the well being of everyone in the community and that it has the will and the means to make a difference to their lives.

There is, accordingly, no separation in people's minds between church and everyday life – the two are closely related – and this is an understanding which, I believe, we have lost sight of in Britain as the Church has become increasingly seen as concerned purely with spiritual values. Such a view is unfair, as many individual Christians, parishes, dioceses and church organisations in Britain are quite clear that 'spiritual values' include the well-being and physical circumstances of people, and not merely those people who attend church. But whenever a Bishop stands up in the House of Lords to contribute to a debate which is seen as a purely secular matter he is told by our predominantly secular press to stick to religious issues and leave day to day life to those whose concern it is. There is no such separation of interests in Mara.

Women's Co-operative, Bunda

New tenant, Bunda

Chapter 4
Discipleship & Mission

Mara's Discipleship and Development Programme (DDP) began in 2004. It is an innovative attempt to synthesise spiritual and practical elements in its outreach to people and is led by Rhobi, whose infectious laughter and bubbly personality make a visitor feel that something good is going to happen soon. She says that the DDP's long term objective is 'to encourage and equip Christians in Mara both spiritually and physically so that by their lives, words and deeds they will be powerful witnesses of Jesus.' In the short term the DDP provides appropriate support, expert advice, start-up funding and monitoring so that projects are successfully launched and completed alongside continuing discipleship through bible study.

In contrast to the projects described earlier, Rhobi's interventions are targeted at Christian groups, so they are parish based and offered through the parish network, with the active co-operation of the *Mchungaji*, or Pastor concerned. The word '*mchungaji*' has the literal meaning of 'shepherd' (though it can also mean 'cowherd' or 'goat herd' according to the species in question) and is in daily, ordinary use in predominantly rural Mara. This distinguishes it from 'Vicar', or even 'Pastor' which in Britain have purely church connections, and which identify their bearers as someone whose emphasis will be principally religious in the narrow sense of that word. The '*Mchungaji*', however, is seen and experienced as one who will protect and lead his flock through all the vicissitudes of life, so even by word association he has a head start on his British counterpart as far as credibility is concerned.

Rhobi had agreed to take me to some of the projects currently active but on the day itself I discovered that her car had broken down in Mugumu, 85 miles away from her office. The projects have to be visited, however, in order to ensure continuous monitoring, and so I went with Benjamin, a driver on the diocesan team. Today, he was upgraded to be my guide and we were to be driven by Laddi again.

Prayers completed, we set off for Kirumi, no more than 45 minutes away and most of it on the tarmac road. We paused at a crossroads and were immediately surrounded by numbers of young women and girls all thrusting produce at us in the hope that we would take advantage of the lower prices than we would pay in town. They may have walked many miles to this spot in the hope of selling some of their surplus tomatoes, bananas, mangoes, peppers, peanuts, sweet potatoes, onions and maize cobs. We selected one or two items to the delight of a lucky few and turned off into the bush. We were immediately faced with a bewildering choice of trails, with no evidence of wheeled traffic at any point. A group of surly looking baboons moved reluctantly out of our path at the last minute, for all the world like a truculent gang of teenagers unwilling to cede territory. The tracks meandered through low scrub and a few stunted acacia trees. The soil was sandy, and unsuitable for cultivation, so could be used for nothing other than grazing.

African goats in particular can scratch a living from anything that grows or has grown, no matter how unpalatable. They can even survive in town, where discarded newspaper is an appetising treat.

Laddi swung confidently from one unmarked track to another, and we eventually pulled up in front of a tin roofed, brick built church with a thatched vicarage nearby and one or two small huts close to it. There was a solar panel on the vicarage roof and Benjamin told me that every vicarage in the diocese now has one of these. This gives the *mchungaji* the opportunity to read after dark, and also confers a measure of status. The panels are installed and serviced by Benjamin himself, who turns out to be the diocesan 'Bwana Solar' as well as a driver.

We went into the church and were met by the Vicar, Nelson, dressed in a smart suit as he was later to attend a seminar in Musoma. A number of parishioners were already there, waiting for our arrival. Nelson led us in prayer, and we went through extended introductions, then set off to look at the project we had come to see. We went on foot, following the line of the overhead electricity cables carried by lofty pylons bearing power to Musoma – power which is tantalisingly close but totally inaccessible to the villages below. We made our way over the sandy tracks and as we rounded a bend we saw a structure ahead, raised on stilts and made of wooden slats. We went closer and saw that it was full of animals, who were peering at us through the gaps, as full of curiosity as I was myself. "This is our sheep project," Nelson said, with obvious pride. The raised platform protected them from foot rot and provided an airy and healthy environment. I asked how they came to make such a different kind of structure and a spokesman told me that all the know-how came from the Church. It looked a bit on the improvised side and bore a strong resemblance to the goat shed I had seen before in Bunda with the ICDP. The wisdom of using local materials and skills is borne out by the many failed projects which litter Africa where high tech innovations have led to inevitable breakdown and abandonment for want of spares or expertise. This is something that they have made themselves and which they can readily service without help from outside.

Knowing that the DDP offers a choice of projects, I asked them how this one was selected for them. "We chose it ourselves," they said, "because we thought this was something we could manage." The project is now five years old and they clearly *are* managing. Sheep can produce offspring annually and the original five provided by the diocese have multiplied at a gratifying rate. There are twenty-four occupants of the pen at present, but the objective of the enterprise is to raise income, and many have already been sold for meat. They have even managed to buy a cow with the profit made to date and they said that they aim to add more to the herd as the project continues to prosper. I asked them if they had any way of making extra income before this project started and learned that they used to make *jamvi*, the bamboo matting sold in UK garden centres as decorative screening. Here they are used as sleeping mats, but they are low value and so nowhere near as lucrative a project as sheep. Were there a B&Q in Musoma, it might be a different story.

The parishioners were clearly happy to be on an upward curve in their way of life and to see an improved future ahead for themselves and their children. I asked them how they have used the profits so far and learned that as well as buying more sheep and a cow they have managed to pay their *Mchungaji's* stipend and also supported a number of orphaned children in the area. On the way back to church they talked about their other farming activities and told me that many of their crops were eaten by zebras last year and that two elephants destroyed one plot within an hour. Such casually told catastrophes bring home what a gulf of experiences lies between our two countries.

Seated once more on the home-made benches in church I asked them about the discipleship part of the deal with the Church. They told me about the seminars with which the project began five years ago and explained that the idea for a community enterprise came from their bible studies.

"Before the diocese came here," they said, "we didn't meet together very often. We didn't even eat together, but now we do and we see that it is better to work together than to struggle on alone."

"Are there any other benefits that you see from such meetings?" I asked.

"Yes," they replied. "Soon after the first meeting we started a Sunday School for our children and then we began to make house to house visits in our village, encouraging others to join us and making sure that people were not ill or in need of some kind."

"So do you think the parish is a better place now than it was five years ago?" There was a loud chorus of agreement at this point and Pastor Nelson intervened.

"There is no doubt about that," he said. "They were without a pastor for six months before I arrived, but what I found was a strong parish with everyone helping each other and a lot of activity. Working together has been good for us."

I asked them if they had questions for me and, not unexpectedly, they began to list a number of requirements. They were modest – money for a few hand tools to help them in their farming activities. They are aware that any European that arrives in such a remote spot is incalculably wealthy in their terms and also, that he is probably well disposed. Nelson broke in again and said that this meeting was not about money, but about their spiritual development.

"Money comes to an end," he said, "but things of the spirit last forever." I felt they were not too impressed with this dusty answer, but Benjamin then jumped to his feet and said that I was not the right person to ask for help with agricultural problems.

"We have a Development Department in Musoma," he pointed out. "You can always bring your problems to us there and we can find the best solution to them, working together." I admired his skill at pointing them back to the Church as a one-stop shop for all their needs – physical and spiritual.

I thanked them for their time and we finished, of course, with prayer before adjourning for lunch. Whilst waiting for the food to be made ready I sat in the shade of a nearby tree and talked to the local carpenter who was making a door for the church. His first job was to construct his own workbench fixed to the tree where I was sitting, and he obligingly posed for a photo. Food was then announced and we all moved back into the multi-purpose church.

We prayed again and I examined the food. It was small, bony fish served in tiny dishes, and with a large plate of ugali for us all to tear chunks from. Not my preferred option, and as there were no implements on offer I struggled to match their expertise in making small spoons of the stiff ugali maize flour paste with which to scoop up the sauce in which the fish were lying. The African way to deal with bony fish is to 'let your mouth do the work' then spit out the residue, but this is an art I have yet to master, so much of the protein in my meal went to waste, almost certainly to mild disapproval from my hosts. Whilst this was not my favourite meal of the week I was aware that, as always, we guests had been given the best available. Hospitality is a key feature of life in Mara.

We eventually got on our way, aiming for the Parish of Magatini and were bowling along at a good rate discussing the morning's experiences when, suddenly, the car began to swing wildly all over the road, with Laddi struggling to regain control of the wheel. We screeched to a halt and climbed out. Conversation switched instantly from discipleship to motor mechanics.

The rear nearside wheel had locked solid and we stared at the wavy skid mark that charted our progress for the last hundred yards. Laddi is a qualified mechanic as well as a driver and he confidently jacked up the Landcruiser and removed the wheel to take a look. Unfortunately, he had no tools with him, other than a wheel brace and jack handle. He used the wheel brace to give the drum a few optimistic bangs, augmented by a number of whacks with a stone picked up at the side of the road. Nothing moved, and we scratched our heads, exchanging a few sage remarks about seized brakes and other mechanical malfunctions beyond my vocabulary range.

It seemed like stalemate, but then a motorcycle pulled up behind us and its smiling rider greeted Laddi warmly. They are old friends and Laddi claims to have taught him all he knows about car mechanics. The pupil turned out to be more provident than his master, however, as he had a large bag of tools on his carrier. The first one he pulled out was, disappointingly, a hammer and he used it to take a few more experimental swings at the offending drum. When brute force produced no results he resorted to science and an assortment of spanners and screwdrivers was brought into play. After an hour's sweaty endeavour, the wheel was pronounced fit for purpose, and we set off again, rather more cautiously this time, for Magatini.

We soon left the mud road and set off across the bush, through areas of black cotton soil good for agriculture but perilous for drivers with even a spoonful of rain, which transforms it into slippery grease with no hope of traction. We scanned the sky anxiously for clouds, but saw only a bright yellow sun in an endless blue sky. We eventually swung into Magatini and saw that there was a large crowd of men and women, some hundred strong, waiting patiently for us under a huge, spreading Jacaranda tree. Most were sitting on the ground, or on rocks, but one or two were on chairs, which were quickly vacated for us, the guests.

This was the Gender Issues group, started by the Diocese in February 2012, so just a year old on my visit. They had been waiting for us all day and we had, first, to apologise for our over-long stay at Kirumi, and then our mishap on the road. Apologies accepted with good grace, the meeting began and I was introduced to the group. I was becoming adept at establishing that I had 'nothing in my pockets' and that I was there to learn, rather than to teach or to distribute largesse. This settled, they began to explain the group's purpose, and it ranged over a number of subjects, all to do with challenging traditional practices inimical to girls' and women's well-being.

First, they talked about education and openly admitted that they previously did not see the value in educating girls beyond primary level. 'How will that help her in her daily life' had been the commonly held view – one that we don't have to go back too far in our own society to recognise. With leadership and encouragement from the DDP they have learned to discuss this issue at length and to agree that times change and if they want to keep up with them, they, too, must change. They have started within their own group to make sure that girls have the same opportunities as boys, and have extended this into their own church teaching groups as well.

The next topic was more controversial, and to do with ownership.

"In the old times," one speaker said, "If there was a bicycle in the house, it belonged to the husband. If there was a sewing machine, it belonged to the husband. Cows? They belonged to the husband. The house itself? The husband's. But now we are getting used to the idea that such things are shared, and that the wife, too, has property rights."

This was impressive, and when we moved onto the next topic – violence – it was even more so. They gave some graphic examples of how women have suffered at the hands of men, and not only the hands. Sticks, knives and even fire were identified as weapons that have been used against women and they said, with some feeling, that there has traditionally been nobody to whom they could complain – it was just the way of the world.

"But now there is," one woman member said. "Any woman can now come to us, and we will deal with it." The whole emphasis of their presentation to me was on changed behaviour, and there seemed to be a high degree of consensus amongst them that this is a good thing, and that the Church has brought it about.

The final topic was the most controversial of all, and one I never expected to see aired in such a public forum – female genital mutilation. In this area it has been traditionally carried out at the age of seven to nine, and has always been considered an essential part of a woman's growing to maturity.

The advent of AIDS has been one of the factors that has helped them to question the value of such a tradition as it has become clear that female circumcision has helped its spread. This is because the practice is coupled with the loss of blood and use is often made of one instrument for a number of operations. Also, researchers now believe that due to damage caused by the operation, subsequent sexual intercourse can result in lacerations of tissues, which greatly increase the risk of transmission.

As a result of this group's new thinking, two local practitioners in Magatini have now come round to the belief that it is a tradition that can be abandoned, but there are others who are still to be convinced, and the parishioners now believes that it is part of their job to do the convincing.

This sort of challenge to deep rooted tradition is not without problems, and there have been families torn between adhering to the old ways and taking up the new. Some young women have listened to the new teaching and decided it suits their natural inclinations, but have been prevailed upon by their parents to submit. Some such girls have resisted parental pressure and even run away to avoid it, and this has presented the Church with the responsibility of how to care for them.

When I asked how these new ideas have come about they pointed immediately to the initial seminars brought to the parish by the DDP. "After all," they told me, "there is no justification in the bible for treating women as being of less worth than men!"

The issues having been aired, we moved onto the second element of this initiative – dancing! A group of young men and women lined up opposite each other and began to gyrate in a suggestive dance routine that simulated unambiguously close relationships between them as they sang and swayed towards each other. I didn't understand the words of the song as they were using the local Kuria language rather than Swahili. They were accompanied by musicians playing home-made traditional instruments. There was a primitive harp, a susaphone-like wind instrument, and a percussion player who had metal containers strapped to his legs, filled with pebbles which rattled as he moved in time to the music and the dance.

It was all highly entertaining, but what had it got to do with the project, I wondered. They laughed at my question and explained that the songs were all about the issues we had been discussing.

"What good does it do to cut up your young girls?" was the sort of challenge being thrown out by the dancers, and people who may not respond to a lecture were given something to think about in a different way.

Then we moved to Part III – electricity. They took me over to a small building with a solar panel mounted on the roof. Inside there was a row of mobile phones having their batteries charged. Now, as it seems, that every Tanzanian has a mobile, those far from the national grid are not content to be cut off from friends, family and bank manager by a flat battery. The parish of Magatini has started this modest income generating project to meet that need. And of the need there is no doubt. During our long meeting under the tree, I was constantly aware of a variety of mobile ring tones going off around me and did wonder if this most welcome of modern developments has been a factor in helping new ideas take hold.

The solar panel, along with the expertise to protect and maintain it, had been supplied by the diocese with the aid of a small, low interest loan, It will be interesting to see what such a well motivated group initiates in future and who will come up with similar, viable income generating projects.

It was now time for food again, and we were offered chicken and rice. Always wary of chickens that have spent their lives running around acquiring more stringy muscle than the succulent meat on a Sainsbury's special, I spooned a couple of tiny pieces onto my heaped up rice and poured on a little of the juice in which the chicken was resting. A neighbour protested that I didn't have enough and generously added a sturdy chicken leg to my modest portion. I contrived to thank him gracefully and tackled the chicken leg, but the spoon – the only implement on offer – was inadequate for the task so it was back to fingers again. Once again, we were given the best that was on offer.

Fortunately, as always in Tanzania, we had all been offered hand washing facilities. Holding our hands out over a bowl, we had warm water poured over them until all traces of the day's dusty activities were washed away. The chicken wasn't bad, and the rice was excellent – grown not a hundred yards away in a marshy spot ideally suited to the job, and mercifully free from gravel.

On the way back to Musoma we discussed the day's activities, and particularly the effect on the two relatively recently established parishes of Kirumi and Magatini. The establishment of the Church in each place has made a difference to the whole community by introducing new ideas and challenging long standing customs and beliefs. The DDP's name in Swahili is *Utume na Maendeleo* with 'Utume' standing for Discipleship. Its more everyday translation, however is 'Mission' and it is evident that the linkage between mission and development is central to what the diocese is trying to achieve in its outreach.

Goat house, Kirumi

Gender discrimination group, Magatini

Chapter 5
God is not a stranger

It was 7am at Mara Diocese's Issenye High School and the school 'bell' (a discarded wheel hub which resonates over the whole campus) was announcing the start of morning assembly. The students had, for the last half hour, been sweeping and tidying the classrooms and grounds. (No caretaker or groundsman at Issenye.) It was Friday and, by design, no teachers were present. The early morning temperature was a pleasant 20°C and all 535 uniformed students were arranged outside in a three sided square, the fourth being a covered platform on which a group of girls and boys began to sing a song of their own composition, swaying rhythmically from side to side as they did so.

"This is the time for prayer," they sang, "the time to speak to Jesus and tell him 'we love you.'"

They were applauded and as they moved off to join their classmates, they were replaced by 17 year old Adam, from Form III, who announced that he would read a passage from the Bible. It was Mark 5: 25-34 and there was a pause whilst a number of students turned to the page in their own bibles which they had brought with them. When he came to the end of the passage he began to expound its meaning – all in fluent English, his third language after his tribal Kikuria and national Swahili. He concluded with a final injunction to remember that our prayers are important to Jesus, so we should be diligent in addressing them to him. He was given full and respectful attention throughout. There were no sly nudges, no winks, no whispers, no mocking faces or disrespectful gestures.

Assemblies at Issenye vary throughout the week, and on the following Tuesday all teachers were present and the students lined up this time in front of a saluting base next to a flagpole in front of the central complex of offices and sixth form classrooms. Each year group was individually drilled, standing first to attention and then at ease. The drill sergeant, himself a student, then commanded the flag bearer to approach, and he did so at a brisk march. They saluted each other smartly and the flag bearer fixed a tightly furled flag of Tanzania to a lanyard on the mast. He raised it, slowly and deliberately, then pulled on a cord to release it. As it began to flutter in the breeze, students and teachers began to sing the national anthem, open palms across their breasts, American style. The tune is '*Sikelele Afrika*' shared with South Africa and a number of other countries in this vast continent. Here in Tanzania, however, the words are in Swahili.

"God bless Africa. God bless Tanzania. God bless the children of Tanzania," they sang, then moved on to other songs, asking for God's blessing on them and their school and giving thanks for the new day and its endless opportunities.

I have tried to imagine these two scenes repeated in Britain, but found it difficult. It is not that young people in Britain are without faith. But many of those who have it, or are ready to explore its possibilities, soon learn that any display of religious interest can open them to scorn and ridicule from their peers. Our Sunday Schools, youth organisations and congregations have become reluctantly resigned to losing their young members as they enter their teens and we spend many hours planning and pondering how to lure them back with music, sport and assorted social activities without frightening them off by talking about God. The belief that scientific thought and religious belief are irreconcilable is so well established in Britain, and the consequent tide of secularism so strong that it's a brave young person who is prepared to stand up against it.

Back in Musoma, I was seated in a hefty Landcruiser ready for another visit with the 'Discipleship and Development' team. We began with lengthy prayers asking for God's help on our journey. I always hope at such times that not everything is being left to God and that normal servicing schedules have also been observed, but I kept such irreverent thoughts to myself and was content to be reminded that here in Mara all our efforts throughout the day and at all times are done in God's name.

It was still only nine o'clock in the morning, but this was the third time that I had bowed my head in prayer that day. Giving thanks before eating is routine in Mara, so breakfast was the first occasion. Then, every diocesan day starts with prayers in the cathedral, with all the diocesan workers, cathedral clergy and any visitors in attendance. This constant reference back to the source of our efforts provokes thought and inspiration.

Prayers for a safe journey over, we set off and our driver, Laddi once again, initiated a serious theological discussion about the nature of sin. He posed the question of why, when we all know what we should do, we still fail to do it – even those of us who claim to be Christians. We had a captive vicar in the car for this leg of the journey, and Laddi fastened on to his answers like a terrier with a rat between its teeth – he just wouldn't let go. We got back to basics with Adam and Eve, and the serpent taking the rap, then moved on to where the Garden of Eden was, and what Adam and Eve looked like. 'Were they black, or white?' we debated. Abraham and the Israelites came under discussion and the question of whether Jews and Arabs differ racially. Laddi was astonished but intrigued to hear that Bethlehem is peopled by Christian Arabs and that led us to get on to the theological differences between Christians and Muslims.

Such discussions are part of everyday life in Mara and are not confined to churchgoers. Slogans on buses and lorries reflect a generalised belief in a world of the spirit. This makes the Church itself less of an oddity, which is increasingly the way it is seen in Britain where people outside it, even those who are well disposed to what it stands for, are likely to dismiss Church as an idea which has little or no relevance to their own lives. The church building itself is seen by many as no more than the traditional place to solemnise rites of passage such as baptisms, marriages and funerals.

One wants the church building and its ministers to be there of course, as a suitable back-drop for such occasions, and a personal or a national crisis may provoke an instinctive turning towards it for comfort, but life soon resumes its normal course and for most of the time it is perceived as no more than somewhere for like-minded people to gather on a Sunday, sing hymns and enjoy each other's company. Christians are expected to restrict 'God talk' to its place and time – in church and on Sunday. An American President addressing the nation experiences no discomfort when telling his people that 'our thoughts and prayers are with the victims' of whatever disaster has recently befallen, but as Tony Blair's former spin-doctor Alastair Campbell once famously put it – "We don't do God."

But they do 'do God' in Mara and talking about God comes naturally. There is nothing self-conscious or even 'religious' about it – it's just part of everyday life and conversation. Nowhere is God dismissed as an outdated concept for the intellectually stunted or scientifically impoverished.

Perhaps when you do actually 'plough the fields and scatter' and wait anxiously for the soft refreshing rain instead of just holding the concept as a distant folk memory, it all makes more sense. Is it our hymn books and our bible stories that help shut God out of our lives because of their strangeness and old fashioned feel?

Some years ago I was in my friend Baragi's compound in Singisi at the end of a full day visiting his extended family and neighbours. I had arrived shortly after dawn and was now preparing to say goodbye as the sun sank towards the horizon. It's always a busy time as the young herdsmen bring in their charges from the far ranging Serengeti grasslands where they have been feeding all day. They are gathered into the safety of a towering thorn hedge, constantly kept in good repair to keep out predators. Predators can be human. Maasai people have the theologically convenient belief that God granted them the custodianship of all cattle, so by relieving their non-Maasai neighbours of theirs, they are doing no more than their religious duty. Baragi is a Taturu, so does not share that view. He also falls asleep each night to the sound of hyenas calling across the plain, and knows that his precious flocks would make them a tasty supper.

First to come in were the cows, trotting in at speed and responding noisily to the plaintive cries of their calves clamouring for their turn at the udder. Then came the sheep and the goats, all pushing in together in a bleating cloud of dust. Baragi dexterously separated them into their respective species; sheep this way, goats that, and the biblical image sprang instantly to life. It was even more telling than it would be at home, where sheep and goats are markedly different from each other. In Africa they are virtually indistinguishable to European eyes but for one significant difference - a sheep's tail hangs down, but a goat's points stiffly skywards.

How vividly the Bible speaks to people in Mara! All the images that Jesus used to illustrate his teaching were drawn from real life and, as he was speaking in the Palestine of two thousand years ago they were predominantly agricultural and pastoral. In our overwhelmingly industrial and commercial society they have to be interpreted to be fully understood. Most of us do not separate sheep and goats on a daily basis, nor do we sow seeds on stony ground, but in Mara they do.

The daily available image of men casting nets out of their boats on Lake Victoria equates perfectly to similar activities on Galilee two thousand years ago and fallen women may still be encountered at the well.

There is consequently no need for the stories to be 'unpacked' for the majority of people of Mara because they are living essentially similar lives to those who crowded round Jesus to hear his life-changing message. The Jesus of the Bible speaks directly to them without any of the '*What Jesus meant by this…..*' explanations that we have become accustomed to in Britain.

By seeming to belong to another age, where everything was different, has God has become a stranger to us? Not in Mara!

Lorry driver's message – 'Nuru ya Mungu'
(*The Light of God*)

Chapter 6
The ABC of AIDS

The first three cases of AIDS in Tanzania were diagnosed in 1983. In the thirty years since then it has come to rival malaria as a major cause of death. It destroys families, and affects mortality rates, literacy, food production and progress of every kind. The sexually active are also the drivers of the economy and Tanzania, like all sub-Saharan countries, is suffering grievously. With mother to child infection on the increase, child mortality rates are also up. The combined efforts of government, NGOs and faith-based organisations, whilst devouring resources which could well be put to other uses, have had only a limited impact on this debilitating disease.

Mara Diocese has established the AIDS-ABC programme, which follows the Tanzanian government's guidelines about how to treat the condition, and is aware of its declared aim of reducing the incidence of AIDS to zero by the year 2017. History suggests that this is an optimistic target, but the diocese now has twelve years of solid experience in this field and, with the government's enthusiastic consent and co-operation, is testing, treating, counselling and helping thousands of people in and around Musoma, the biggest conurbation in Mara, and whose population is most affected by AIDS.

ABC in Mara stands for Awareness, Behaviour and finally Counselling, rather than Condoms as in other organisations. The diocese has not set itself against the use of condoms, and it even gives advice on their availability and effective use, but its stance on moral behaviour before marriage and on 'one partner' relationships means that it is not prepared to promote their use.

I set off with Lucy, one of the diocesan AIDS support workers. We were to see three families with members already diagnosed and living with HIV/AIDS. We first visited Rehema, whose husband was diagnosed fifteen years ago. She looked thin and tired but she greeted us with a delighted smile and a warm invitation to join her. She brought low stools out for us to sit in the shade of a large pawpaw tree, heavy with fruit.

Lucy introduced me and, because of the sensitivity of the subject, I was nervous about asking questions. But Rehema was ready to talk, and the first thing she told me was that the AIDS-ABC programme has greatly reduced the stigma that was formerly attached to the condition. I asked her how that has been achieved and she talked about the choirs, meetings and 'road shows' that are continually giving out the message that AIDS cannot be caught by shaking hands or sharing food or by any other normal activity outside of sexual contact.

As a visitor, I was struck throughout my time in Mara by how openly everyone is ready to talk freely and without embarrassment about AIDS, in marked contrast to how it still seems in Britain where it is thought of as something that happens elsewhere and probably just to homosexuals.

"People are learning that those of us with AIDS are just like anybody else, with the same needs and the same hopes for a normal life," Rehema continued, and she went on to talk about other, practical ways in which the programme has helped her.

"We hear the Word of God," she began, "and this teaches us that we are all precious to God, who loves each and every one of us. We also get advice, medicines, small loans from time to time, and we even got help with building a water tank to catch rainwater from the roof."

She showed me the cement tank built by a team of volunteers from the 'GoMAD' team. (More about them later.) I asked about the loans and she said the Church recently lent her money to buy shoes. She had to explain what the money was for, and was then obliged to use it in the way she said she would. She paid it back after selling a few chickens. I admired her small raised bed stuffed full of herbs and salad crops, which one of Lucy's colleagues from the AIDS-ABC Programme showed her how to build.

"We do have a small *shamba*," she said, "but it is a long way off because we are in town, but now I can grow a few things close to the house, and that is a help." She broke off a leaf of Aloe Vera from a row of plants lining the path and rubbed it between her fingers. It makes a useful cream which is good for skin conditions and itchy eyes. She has also been taught how to raise chickens and ducks, so has meat and eggs to supplement her diet, along with lessons in nutrition that help her to make the most effective use of what she has.

Whilst we were talking, a small girl was with us, staring with open curiosity at the pale stranger come to visit her. I asked Rehema how many children she had. Her face fell and tears sprang to her eyes.

"We don't have any, now," she answered, dully.

AIDS has robbed her of the most precious thing in life – a family. She explained that the child I thought was her daughter belongs to a neighbour, but that she is 'on loan' so as to help her feel more normal and stand out less from those around her.

Lucy asked after Rehema's husband. He was out in the town teaching about AIDS at a seminar run by a club started by the Church and whose members are all people living with AIDS and surviving, with the sort of help Rehema had been describing. In this way, the work that AIDS-ABC has started will survive the programme itself, and a body of knowledge about hygiene, nutrition, self-sufficiency and behaviour will be planted in the community.

We prepared to leave, and Lucy assured Rehema that she will be back as usual, in a month's time. She urged her to encourage others to follow the advice she had been given and reminded her about the importance of boiling her drinking water.

Our next visit was to a compound sitting high above the River Mara estuary, before it empties into Lake Victoria. We moved towards the outskirts of Musoma and the dwellings were more spaced out, with land to till around each household. We had come to visit Asteria, another of Lucy's clients, but as we drew close, calling out greetings, it seemed clear that she was out, and there was no answer. Lucy said this was good news, and explained that when she first came across Asteria she was bedfast and unable to care for herself. The fact that she is now up and about is all the evidence she needs that things are improved, and the signs of such improvement were all around us.

Asteria's road to economic recovery has been through the creation of a profitable chicken project and the very business-like hen coop and wire netting enclosure in front of us had been built with help and advice from the Church. Next to it was a half-built house made of fired bricks and this, Lucy said, had been financed entirely through the sale of chickens and eggs. It will soon replace the traditional mud and thatch hut that stands next to it, and is a further sign of hope and of progress.

Asteria's health issues were stabilised by the use of antiretroviral drugs (ARVs) supplied by the government but distributed by the Church. This medication had been followed up with continuing health care and advice on diet, nutrition and hygiene. Lucy says that there is no problem with access to ARVs, but that the government is relying on the Church, with its network of community contacts and volunteers, to make them available to those in need. Recently, however, a local manufacturer was found to be selling fake ARVs which had no effect other than to give false reassurance to the users.

We pressed on, moving back closer to town and weaving our way through Musoma's dusty suburbs. We had to swerve at one point as a motorcycle approached us with a coffin strapped across its carrier, making it as wide as a car. We eased past it and then pulled up at our destination and were greeted by Athumani, an elderly man squatting cross-legged on the ground and hammering rivets into a metal cooking vessel. His wife sat close by and, once again, we were greeted like old friends. They were effusive about the help they have had from the AIDS-ABC programme and said what a difference it had made to their lives, which they had at one time thought to be over.

But they talked about far more than sheer survival. Once stabilised on drugs they have now been helped to establish their futures with supplies of soap, a mosquito net, food and advice on every aspect of their lives and even help to build a serviceable toilet. Athumani's metal working is the family's money generating project and the basis of their current prosperity. Lucy helped him to buy the tools of his trade and now finds him customers on her travels about town.

Most of all, however, they are grateful for the help with school fees for their surviving son, now eighteen, who is set to enter teacher training college this year. There was, once again, a small child in attendance; not their own but very much at home. She said nothing the whole of the time we were there, but I was mesmerised as I watched her carefully trimming her fingernails with half a rusted razor blade. Health and Safety has yet to reach Mara.

Back at the diocesan offices, a young couple were waiting outside the consulting room. They were engaged to be married and the Church runs a programme whereby couples come for testing once they have made the decision to marry. It was their second visit and, having both proved negative six months ago, they had now returned for another test. If this, too, proved negative, they would have another six months to wait for a third test, after which they will be declared safe to marry. All they have to do then to avoid AIDS is remain faithful to each other.

In the afternoon Richard, the AIDS-ABC co-ordinator, took me to watch one of the programme's 'road shows'. We went to Misisi, about two hours' drive from Musoma and far from any proper road. The show was timed for late afternoon in order to attract people after the day's work was over.

When we arrived, however, some of Richard's team members were already in action, heads down with a group of community volunteers and motivators who receive no reward other than a bicycle to help them get around the villages, and food on road show days. Also present were local government health workers and, together, they were exchanging information and planning the afternoon's activities.

We moved on to the village centre, where speakers had been set up on the roof of a diocesan Landcruiser. The village pulsated to music loud enough for me to feel the vibrations it generated. It was a tuneless chant which may have been rap. Meanwhile, other volunteers were erecting a sturdy gazebo. A crowd of about 90 people had gathered, listening to the music and watching the preparations with interest.

When all was ready, the music was switched off, and the silence was abruptly deafening. AIDS-ABC team member Christopher knew how to deal with that. He took a microphone and wandered about amongst the crowd conducting short interviews, which were all relayed over the massive speakers. Christopher is one of those people for whom microphones were invented, and despite the gravity of the subject, he soon had his audience in a laughing, happy mood with quick banter and repartee. He repeatedly emphasised that, whilst AIDS cannot be cured, it can be prevented. He went on to add that, with help, it can also be lived with, and that people can have normal lives if they listen to the advice and counselling that is freely available to them. He stressed that the diocese makes no charge for any of its AIDS services.

Once they were warmed up, Christopher said that the only way to find out if you have the condition is to be tested. I wondered how anyone from this village could be expected to go for testing in distant Musoma, but then discovered what the gazebo was for. Test kits were produced from the back of the Landcruiser and another team member started to make a list of names as customers began to queue for their turn.

They went into the gazebo one by one and, amazingly, I was invited to witness the procedure, which was impressive. It was a one-to-one talk with questions about life style readily answered and assurances given that, whatever the result, it is better to know than to go on in ignorance and hope for the best. The motherly looking nurse giving the advice inspired confidence and confidences as she talked calmly and listened sympathetically to each one. She praised a 20 year old unmarried mother with a child on her hip for coming forward and encouraged her to be an adviser and example to others of her age group, identifying her as a potential team member and 'youth ambassador'.

This element of community involvement and empowerment runs through all the Church's projects. Target clients are not simply 'treated' but are recruited for training on issues such as HIV/AIDS transmission, leadership, good governance, and human rights using criteria set by the programme. In the same way, gender equality is encouraged by giving equal chances to both women and men to be trained and supported, with the aim of reducing the acceptability and incidence of domestic violence in the targeted communities.

Thirty-eight men and women were tested in all at this road show, which Richard said was quite a small one. Two hundred can be tested on some days. Of today's thirty-eight, three were tested positive. This represents almost 8%, slightly above the average for Mara Region as a whole. Everyone was then given a comprehensive booklet about HIV/AIDS and told about the centre at diocesan headquarters in Musoma where anyone can come for help.

As the last few customers were seen, dark thunder clouds blotted out the evening sun and we raced to dismantle the gazebo and cover the speakers before the rain came shuttering down and dispersed the crowd to their homes. Thirty-five families could now breathe more easily and make decisions about future behaviour. Three have much talking to do, but in the knowledge that they need not stand alone in their changed circumstances. The Church is there to help.

The United Nations is relatively upbeat about AIDS these days. It says that, globally, there were 700,000 fewer new HIV infections in 2011 than in 2001, and Africa has cut AIDS-related deaths by one third in the past six years. It talks about the 8 million people now on ARVs, but goes on to say that a further 7 million still have no access to them. *(UNAIDS World Aids Day Report for 2012.)*

Tanzania's infrastructure is still so poor that it lags behind most of its neighbours in delivery of services of every kind, and relies heavily on faith organisations and other NGOs to do its work. To its credit, the Government is ready to collaborate fully with the Church and it is a partnership which brings the possibility of a future to people who had previously lost all hope.

AIDS-ABC works in phases and the immediate aim (in March 2013) was to raise awareness about harmful traditions in relation to the spread of HIV and AIDS among no fewer than a precisely targeted 25,219 people in a specific geographical area. This was to be achieved within a two year period, and as a result of careful record keeping they could tell me that 11,978 people had already been reached. This was done through meetings, training seminars, 'road shows', and the recruitment of community volunteers.

A secondary objective was to reduce the incidence of stigma among the HIV infected and the open way in which the programme's clients were prepared to talk to me about it indicates that Lucy and her colleagues are winning that particular battle.

The AIDS-ABC programme is universally admired in Mara and the government officials I spoke to were full of praise for the Church's role in mitigating the effects of this life-changing condition. As for the programme's clients, the love and commitment shown to them by Lucy and her colleagues was matched by deep seated gratitude and huge appreciation. It would be difficult to get closer to the Jesus model of service than this. People are not being told about the love of God – they are being shown it.

Cheerful queue for HIV test, AIDS-ABC Road Show

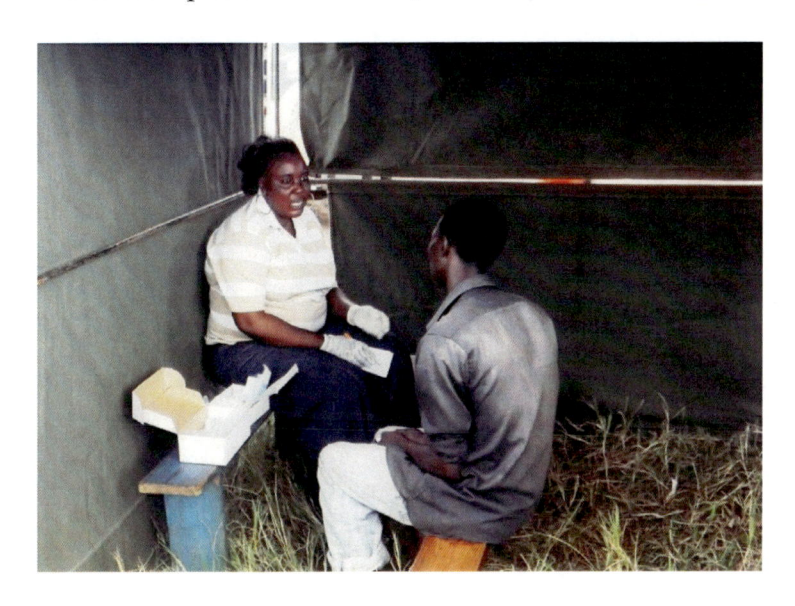

Counselling, AIDS-ABC Road Show

Chapter 7
Dangerous wildlife

Mara has lions, spitting cobras, elephants, crocodiles, and a diverse menagerie of animals that are potentially dangerous to human life, but it is *dudus* that pose the greatest risk. '*Dudu*' is a Swahili word which the dictionary usually renders as 'insect,' but as it can be applied to spiders, worms and even small snakes, 'creepy crawly' is the best fit and Africa has lots of them. The tropical climate ensures that they are both numerous and from a European perspective, rather big. Butterflies and spiders come the size of birds, and beetles look like heavily armoured mice.

    I was reflecting on this on my bed in the 'Savoy' after a long day greeting old friends and commiserating on the family deaths that had occurred since last we met. I could hear a hyena in the distance casting its echoing *whoop* across the Serengeti when a sudden movement caught my eye and I saw an enormous cockroach shouldering its way across the floor from some unseen hiding place. I have been told that cockroaches, despite their ability to cause the instant closure of any food outlet in Britain, have never yet been found to transmit any disease. This does not make me like them. One trusts that Noah knew what he was doing when he let two of them into the Ark, but my bedroom is a space too far. I swatted this one quickly out of the door, no doubt to invade my possibly more accommodating neighbour's space.

The next intruder was a gecko. About the size and shape of a newt, he was a more welcome guest, and was consequently accorded squatting rights. Geckoes are endlessly entertaining because of their remarkable ability to walk unconcernedly upside down across the ceiling. I used to believe they had tiny suction pads on their feet, but now understand that this skill is down to a small electric charge they generate which enables them to defy gravity. If they lose their concentration and switch off, however, they do come crashing down and land with a faint splat. They are also fascinating hunters. Having located their prey they wait, motionless and beady-eyed, for long minutes before darting in, quick as lightening, for a fast kill.

These harmless bit players are overshadowed by Africa's most deadly *dudu* - the tiny mosquito, with its unique ability to transmit malaria, which is a major public health problem in Tanzania, with annual deaths estimated to be 60,000. According to USAID's *President's Malaria Initiative*, approximately 14 to 18 million cases of malaria are reported annually by Tanzanian public health services and more than 40% of all outpatient visits are attributed to malaria. Many more cases are neither reported nor recorded.

Tanzania's malaria is of the falciparum variety, the deadliest form of the disease, responsible for 90% of deaths from malaria worldwide. Other forms of malaria occur in India and elsewhere which are milder in effect but which can recur over years and even decades. Falciparum does not recur; the patient either dies or recovers until the next contact with a parasite bearing mosquito. Young children are particularly at risk, with 80 per cent of deaths occurring among those under five years of age. Can we imagine how we would feel about 4,000 young children dying from one disease *every month*? For those who survive, malaria is an extremely unpleasant experience, and for adults it makes work impossible, leaving the sufferer weak and lethargic.

The male mosquito is harmless enough, feeding on sugar which he extracts from plant nectar. The female does that too, but when she needs to lay eggs she has to have blood, which she acquires by the antisocial practice of sticking her proboscis into us and drawing out blood which then travels into her abdomen. Her saliva contains a protein that prevents blood from clotting and leaves behind an itchy bump. If that were all, it would be no more than an irritation, but the mosquito has a sting in her tail or more accurately, in her nose. In the process of fulfilling her maternal duty she also, if she has been infected with malarial parasites, shares them with us. If we are lucky, she will not have been so infected, and all we get is the itchy bump.

If infected, however, her bite injects young forms of the malaria parasite into our blood. The parasites travel through the bloodstream to the liver, where they grow to their next stage of development. In six to nine days, they leave the liver and enter the bloodstream again. They invade the red blood cells, finish growing, and begin to multiply quickly. The number of parasites increases until the red blood cells burst and are destroyed, releasing thousands of parasites into the bloodstream. They attack other red blood cells, and the cycle of infection continues, causing the common signs and symptoms of malaria, including anaemia which is particularly dangerous for young children.

So where do mosquitoes pick up their infection? The answer is – from us. When a non-infected mosquito bites an infected person, she sucks up parasites along with the blood which she needs to survive. That mosquito is then infected with the malaria parasites which then go through several stages of growth in the mosquito. When the mosquito bites someone else, that person then becomes infected with malaria parasites, and the cycle begins again. So, we get malaria from mosquitoes, but they get it from us, and it's the parasites that should take the blame rather than the humble mosquito who is simply doing what she has to do to survive.

The Church in Mara takes malaria seriously. I set off from Musoma in one of Mara's four wheel drive Landcruisers travelling deep into Mjita country, south of Musoma and often within sight of Lake Victoria. The landscape alternated between massive granite outcrops with tiny homesteads nestling in their shadow and open plains dotted with stately mango trees offering welcome shade and the promise of succulent fruit to come.

Arthur Mauya, Mara's Director of Education and Wakefield Link Officer, was at the wheel and he became increasingly nervous as we moved into an area which had evidently experienced recent and heavy rain. Some sections of the mud road had been well maintained, but as we reached less frequently used tracks we were repeatedly forced to avoid areas where other vehicles had left deep, water-filled holes and we inched our way round them. Arthur's nervousness was explained when he told me that he became immovably stuck here on his last visit. He only broke free by hiring two teams of oxen, eight animals in all, to pull him out of the sticky mud. So, although that would be a memorable photograph for the album, I now shared his nervousness and gladly approved of his decision to abort the journey if things got much worse.

We persevered, however, and our destination finally came into sight – a village primary school. We were only just in time as it was Friday afternoon before the Easter holiday and the six hundred or so children were assembled, ready to be dismissed. The classrooms were the usual dismal collection of broken down structures, with crumbling walls, rusty roofs and little furniture. The children were sitting outside on the ground, under the shade of strategically planted trees.

We were greeted warmly by the teachers, who immediately vacated chairs for us, and Arthur explained that we had come from the Anglican Church in Musoma to distribute mosquito nets to the children. Their school had been chosen as the money for the nets came from St Andrew's Church in Wakefield, linked with the church in this village, Masinono. He went on to say that the nets were for first and second year children, they being the most vulnerable to malaria. The teachers said that even they themselves didn't have nets, but Arthur said firmly "That's up to the government." The teachers then said "OK, leave the nets with us and we'll distribute them," but Arthur replied, even more firmly, "No that's not how it works."

He turned to the children and embarked on a thorough teaching about malaria and mosquito nets, first drawing out of them what they already knew. He talked about the importance of a clean environment, and explained that even a hoof print or an upturned leaf filled with water can be a breeding ground for mosquitoes. He explained about the 'dusk till dawn' danger period when mosquitoes are active, and told them how international efforts to distribute millions of mosquito nets have brought death figures down. He asked them who knows somebody who has died from malaria, and every hand shot into the air. That done, he lined up all the first years, recorded their names, and gave them a net each which they clutched tightly to their chests. He repeated this with the second years until all the nets had gone. There was excited chatter as they examined their unexpected gifts and we left them to their final Assembly knowing that 120 young children had now been given a fighting chance of achieving maturity.

There is no formal link between school and church in Masinono, and no attempt to limit the distribution of nets to Anglican or even Christian children. As Arthur said on the return journey: "Mosquitoes don't choose whom they will bite, do they?"

Next day I was in the care of Hesbon, one of Mara Diocese's two Malaria Project development officers. Hesbon is a 37 year old Luo man with a deep resonating voice and a ready smile. We talked on the journey and I discovered that the malaria project has an integrated approach and also concerns itself with hygiene and sanitation. We were on our way to check progress at

Chirorwe, where the diocese has installed a 45,000 litre water tank and new latrines at a government primary school.

Half an hour out of Musoma we stopped for breakfast at a grubby little roadside café. We washed our hands at the tap provided at every food outlet in Tanzania and ordered spiced *chai* and freshly made chapattis. It was a second breakfast for me, hobbit-style, and delicious. We set off again, and soon left the tarmac road far behind. After an hour of bumping over the mud and gravel, we reached Chirorwe and turned off into a government primary school, standing amongst shade giving trees. As at Masinono, the buildings were semi-derelict, with termite-ridden roof timbers hanging down over the pupils' heads, mud brick walls crumbling, and neither frames nor glass in the gaping window spaces. Young faces appeared at each hole in the wall, curious to see who had arrived.

The water tank we had come to see stood proudly above ground with its newly finished cement contrasting sharply with everything else in sight. It was finished, but gutters had yet to be fitted to the most recently built and best of the classrooms from whose roof the tank will collect rainwater. We moved on to the new latrines and these, too, were still in pristine condition, almost ready for use. Like the tank, they were of superior construction and had been installed by contractors from Arusha, some 300 miles distant.

We sat on low stools set out beneath a colossal mango tree whose broad leaves provided deep and welcome shade. The Muslim head teacher spoke enthusiastically about the benefits that the new water tank and the latrines will provide for her 530 pupils, and expressed her gratitude to the diocese and to Hesbon, who is clearly well known here, and liked. I was also thanked, and at this point had to make my regular and disappointing admission that I was here on my own behalf and did not bear gifts from a distant benefactor.

We moved into a classroom with the head teacher and a number of her colleagues who abandoned their classes to listen to Hesbon. He told them that they will be able to attend a week of seminars in Musoma where they will receive intensive training in health and hygiene issues from a variety of experts and went on to give them an introductory lesson to whet their appetites.

He circulated a set of beautifully produced A3 laminated pencil drawings, commissioned by the diocese and made by an artist in Musoma. They showed young children in a village setting and displayed 'bad, better and best' practice in a variety of circumstances. The teachers first discussed them in pairs and were then shown how to use them with a class of children. They will receive a duplicate set after completing their training. Hesbon had their undivided attention and, although they took no notes, he is skilled at working in this oral tradition and kept looping back to points made previously in order to reinforce them and establish them in his audience's collective consciousness.

He talked about caring for the new water tank and how the gutters must be kept clean and free of leaves or other debris. He knows that it is lack of maintenance that so often reduces the effect of new installations in Africa.

The latrines should not have soapy water put into them he said, as this can affect the cement from which they are constructed. He moved on to the effectiveness of mosquito nets and the correct way to use them, emphasising all the time that they must *teach* their pupils this knowledge – not just *tell* them about it.

He then raised the question of a financial contribution from the school itself, and at this point the head teacher did start to take notes. Hesbon asked who will benefit from the good supply of water and the shiny new toilets.

'The children,' they answered.

"And who do these children belong to?" he asked.

"The parents," they answered.

"So should they pay something towards the cost?"

They accepted the logic of his argument and agreed to put it to the parents that they should make a contribution, however modest. The head teacher continued to make careful notes. Hesbon went on to make it clear that the teachers must protect their new facilities from being exploited by the wider community. 45,000 litres of water would not go far if all the village were to see it as theirs.

Time for lunch then, and large quantities of rice and fresh fish in tomato sauce were brought out for us. There were no eating implements in sight and I have never mastered the art of using my fingers with which to eat rice, but it was all tasty and nutritious, washed down with factory-bottled water, a comparatively recent but very welcome introduction to Mara.

The teachers then returned to their classrooms, but Hesbon took over in one and this time he produced, not a set of drawings, but a glove puppet with which to make his points. It was obvious that the children had seen the puppet before and they greeted him noisily. He turned out to be a smart puppet who spoke not only Swahili, Kijita and Kijaluo but also, to my surprise, English, French and German. He was also well versed in the control of malaria and basic hygiene and sanitation issues and he enjoyed a good reception from his young audience, several of whom took turns to manipulate him and deliver his message. Hesbon then invited the children to sing for us and they launched into the school song.

"Ours is a good school," they sang. "We will be the ones who build our nation." Their 'good school' roof looked to be in imminent danger of falling on their heads as they sang, the cement floor was breaking up, and the ancient desks were falling apart. Chalked up on a termite-ridden roof beam was the message 'Switch off your mobile', however. The old and the new were sitting comfortably side by side. This is the reality for most primary schools in Mara, and yet from such unpromising starts gifted people like Hesbon himself do emerge and they are, indeed, building the nation.

A number of village elders and government officials had now drifted in. We moved outside again, sitting in the shade but squinting against the fierce light of an African sky. Hesbon embarked on another teaching for the villagers' benefit. He reiterated the stern warnings about use and abuse of the new facilities, then went on to discuss with them issues of malaria, health and hygiene, listening carefully to their ideas and praising them for their willingness to co-operate with the Church and local government officials for the benefit of their school.

At this point, the community choir approached through the trees, singing as they came. They were smartly dressed young men and women, who had been trained by the Malaria Project team, who motivate them by producing a CD for them when they reach an acceptable standard. The first song was one of welcome to Hesbon and me. Then they went on to sing about health and hygiene issues, with special mention of such unlikely themes as diarrhoea, sickness, mosquitoes and AIDS. They finished with a beautifully harmonised but grim warning that there is no cure for the latter so it takes behavioural changes to make a difference.

We thanked them for their contribution and the meeting seemed to be almost over, but Hesbon asked the village elders about a deep pit we had passed, close to the school but apparently abandoned for some time and now overgrown with weeds. They explained that they had intended to build a latrine there, but had run out of enthusiasm. Hesbon urged them to continue with the project, but they said there was nobody who knew how to finish the job. He chided them for making such a wasted effort and asked them if he could put them in touch with the firm of contractors who built the school latrines, and who he knew still had a team in Musoma. They agreed, possibly feeling safe in the knowledge that once Hesbon had gone they could easily forget the idea. But he produced his mobile phone from a pocket and got onto the firm straight away, explaining that he had customers waiting for them in Chirorwe. They agreed to come out next day to make a survey and give a quote. It was a brilliant display of how to exploit the new technology and also how to out-manoeuvre a slow moving committee of village elders.

We left before dusk and I thought gratefully of the mosquito net awaiting me that night, and of the expensive pills I was taking daily to save me from malaria. I also thought about the millions of Tanzanians who would be exposed to malaria before morning through lack of this simplest of protective devices, and access to modern medicines.

Some visitors to Africa have been so affected by the unfairness of this that they have, out of a mistaken sense of solidarity, forsaken the use of a net and given their anti-malarial pills to someone they have befriended. It is well to remember, though, that all Tanzanian adults have been exposed to malaria since childhood, and have acquired some degree of resistance to it, simply by surviving. But when European visitors decide to take the same chance they put themselves in the position of a new born baby, and run exactly the same statistical risk of infection, illness and death.

Health warning: always consult your doctor before visiting sub-Saharan Africa, always take your pills, sleep under a net and use insect repellent. And if you return home with symptoms of fever, sickness or diarrhoea, quickly explain just where you have been.

Free mosquito nets for Standard I

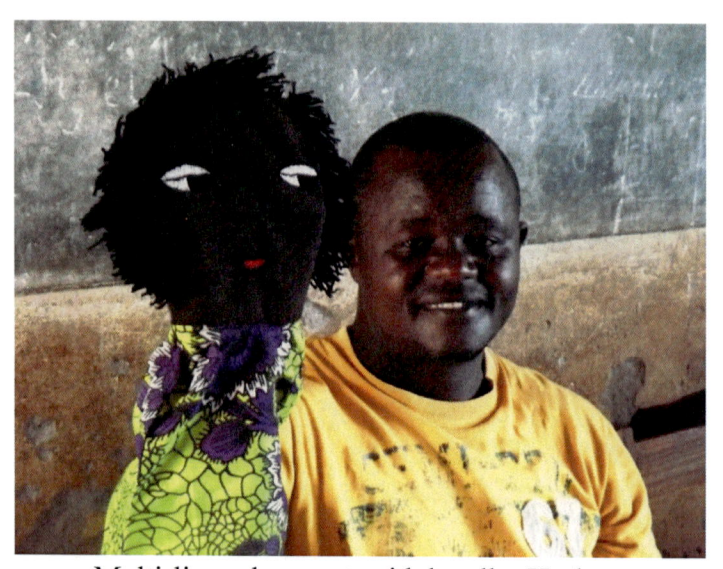

Multi-lingual puppet, with handler Hesbon

Chapter 8
Money, money, money

Because of funding issues, many diocesan programmes in Mara have a precarious future, and their very success creates a growing demand for the services they provide, along with the corresponding expectation that they will continue. There is nothing certain about this. In the second decade of the twenty-first century, most developed countries are experiencing reduced levels of growth, and shrinking numbers of donors are pursued by an increasingly desperate army of applicants. In this climate, the Church's programme directors in Mara spend a significant part of their time trying to secure the continuity of their own project. This exposes an underlying weakness in the model of finance used in Mara, due to its reliance on overseas funding agencies.

What happens is that, through its grassroots contacts at community level, problems such as AIDS, malaria, or unsafe drinking water are identified, and the Church then seeks to address them. A bid is put together, outlining the problem and describing in detail how the Church means to tackle it, with a full costing attached. This bid is then touted round the most likely sources of funding, relying on past experience. If successful, funds are granted and the programme gets under way. There is always a time scale and at the end of the period the programme either folds, an extension is granted, or an alternative donor agrees to pick it up.

Apart from the uncertainty this creates, with the risk of sorely needed programmes such as AIDS-ABC coming to an abrupt end, it also leads to duplication of personnel and other resources, with each project pursuing its goals in accordance with the conditions of the grant. Different diocesan departments do co-operate, sharing personnel, resources and infrastructure when possible, but there is still a parallel tramline feeling about the separate offices, records, accounts and initiatives.

A further negative effect is that this relationship between the donor and the bidder can affect the ability of the project to react to the situation on the ground, for fear of breaking the rules imposed on it by its paymasters. An example of this was exposed when I visited Mara's Community Based Rehabilitation Programme, CBR.

CBR was established in 2001, and it aims to support people with a variety of disabilities. Clinics have been established to treat psychological problems, sight impairment, deafness, speech impediments, cleft palette, club foot, mercury poisoning, and hydrocephalus. Speech therapy, physiotherapy and occupational therapy are also on offer. The clinics are manned by a mixed team of diocesan employees and volunteers, whose efforts are augmented by three field officers who visit families in the surrounding area. All treatment is free, though families do sometimes make voluntary contributions in appreciation of the help they have received.

The well spaced and airy buildings are of top quality, with glazed windows, superior ceiling boards and a good state of decoration. On the day I visited, however, there was only one room in use. In it I was greeted by a group of women who were nursing their young babies, all of whom had various degrees of talipes, commonly known as club foot. At a table at the far end, a young CBR employee, Raymond, was expertly bandaging and plastering a three month old baby's feet in order to coax them into a better position. After a week, he told me, the plaster would be removed and replaced, with additional manipulation to further improve the position of the feet. If caught early enough, this manipulation will eventually effect a complete cure, without the need for surgery. Part of CBR's outreach is to educate parents into bringing in their affected children early on so that this treatment can be started when it is most effective. Without treatment, as the child grows older and heavier, there is increasing distortion of the limbs and physical work becomes impossible – a great hardship in a country where most people still earn a living by cultivating the land.

Older children brought in with this condition are referred to nearby Bunda Hospital where they undergo corrective surgery. Indeed a lot of CBR's work is to identify conditions which it cannot treat itself but which can then be referred to a fully equipped medical facility.

Seeing such skilled and effective work being carried out, I asked why there was only one room in use that day. Dr Henry Yoggo, who directs CBR, explained that all its activities are funded from outside and he cited a list of donors which included USAID, Caritas, and AMREF. He said they are all now tightening their fists and told me that he has had to cut down his staff and can no longer afford even a secretary or a night watchman as he has run out of money with which to pay their salaries.

He appeared deeply frustrated by the attitude of donors whose priorities change. "They are no longer interested in treatment," he said, "but only in awareness raising and prevention."

"That's all very well," he continued, "but we have been raising awareness for many years and once you raise awareness, people who know they need treatment then turn up to ask for it, as well as those to whom we can offer preventive advice."

"Do you have any long term strategy for income generation and eventual self-reliance?" I asked. Again, he told me that he has been thwarted by the attitude of donors to any fund raising initiative. The agency which funded the very fine buildings now in place has stipulated that they cannot be used for commercial activities, so it was a generous gift, but one with strings.

It seems as though donors want to retain control over the gifts they make, rather like the rich uncle who stipulates that the bicycle he gives as a Christmas present should only be used within sight of his own house and ridden at a certain speed. The history of misused funds across Africa makes the donors' concerns understandable. Corrupt political leaders born in mud huts, but who end up with millions of dollars salted away in a Zurich strongroom do not do so by saving up their parliamentary salaries, and church leaders world-wide are not immune to temptation.

But this is not the only reason why donor organisations hang on tightly to purse strings stretched thousands of miles across continents. They also tend to respond to causes which appeal both to them and to the people who provide their money in the first place, whether they be tax payers or charities. The problem with this is that prosaic needs which do not appeal to donors or to their sources of income still require funding, despite their lack of glamour. To put two hypothetical examples, it is comparatively easy to raise money for blind children, but extraordinarily difficult to raise it for vehicle maintenance. An appeal for Braille machines will always win out over one for brake blocks, but the supply of one may depend on the presence of the other. For this reason, money that is not earmarked is the best kind of aid from the recipient's point of view, but it is also the easiest sort to lose track of, which explains donors' caution.

An alternative approach would be for donors to select 'approved partners' on the basis of agreed objectives and procedures, then to allow their gift to be used according to how things are developing on the ground, within the remit of the original agreement. So many factors can change between the articulation of a bid and the execution of its aims that those working at the point of delivery always need a degree of flexibility on expenditure. Once an organisation, such as a diocese, has been declared an approved partner, it could be allowed to get on with it, subject to rigorous external audits, upon whose satisfactory outcome would depend further tranches of aid.

Wakefield Diocese, in its dealings with Mara, has devised a combination of both approaches which has managed to tap into the benefits of each. Firstly, parishioners have been encouraged to respond to specific projects in all three Mara dioceses. Some of these have been at parish level, such as help with building a church or a classroom. These are always popular as it is a natural desire to want to see tangible results as a consequence of one's generosity. Wakefield has always borne the whole cost of administration and this has gone a long way to reassuring those who fear that their gift may be eaten up before it reaches those for whom it was intended. In fact the Church in Mara has a brilliant track record of delivering aid to the point of need to the extent that the Tanzanian government has used it to distribute aid that has come from other sources, in the knowledge that its unrivalled community network can be relied upon to deliver, and that its personnel are likely to have honest motives.

Secondly, those wishing to help Mara but who don't have any specific project in mind have put their contributions into a 'General Fund', which is often described in Mara as a Godsend. Over the last 25 years of the Wakefield-Tanzania Link £277,000 has been sent to the General Fund. This represents 15.8% of the total money sent which stood at £1.75 million in June 2013.

At some point in Tanzania's development, it will be fair to ask why financial help from outside is necessary. How long will it be appropriate for the Church in Africa to rely on subsidies from developed countries in order to deliver its programmes? Until the world is a fairer place and the distribution of wealth is more evenly balanced than at present, that day is far off, but in Mara they are already anticipating it. The problem is well understood at every level of the church hierarchy and beyond. It was first identified as a national policy by Julius Nyerere who rejected the benevolent colonialism implied by the concept of aid in favour of a slower, more organic policy of *kujitegemea*, or self reliance, as part of his dream of a unique brand of 'African Socialism'. That policy survived his retirement in name only, to be replaced with the race for capitalism that is now embraced by virtually every country except North Korea.

But in Mara the Church still treasures the concept of *kujitegemea* and looks forward to the day when it will no longer rely on donors in order to achieve its ends. The irony is that many of its projects deliver badly needed help to the people they target, but also offer opportunities for income generation which would help sustain them. There is much room for development of this notion.

The Community Based Rehabilitation Centre described above is a case in point. The CBR has a ready-made customer base for quality medicines if the diocese were able to turn part of the spacious buildings into a commercial dispensary. As it is, CBR staff prescribe medicines which patients then go and buy elsewhere, allowing others to take the profit. Patients have other needs which could also be provided by the Church. A small café for those who have travelled far could provide additional income, and even overnight accommodation could follow. All would produce a steady flow of income which would then support the excellent and much needed work the CBR does.

Dr Henry sees all this and is enthusiastic about using such methods of raising revenue, which he knows are in place elsewhere in the diocese. He is bound, however, by restrictions laid on him by well meaning donors who have unwittingly slowed down the work they so generously funded at the outset. It is to be hoped that some way of accommodating these differing views will be found. There is a great and growing need for the services that CBR offers and it is unthinkable that the demand the project has identified should go unanswered because of artificial restrictions imposed by well intentioned but far-off donors.

When it comes to raising money from congregational giving, the Church is in the same situation as the country. Just as development in Tanzania is limited by the small yield of its low tax base, so is the Church constrained by the poverty of its members and their consequent inability to make the sort of offering that would enable it to deliver its ambitious programme of health, education and development projects.

This has not stopped the Bishop of Mara taking a robust view on the responsibility of Christians to give until it hurts! When the diocesan synod, for example, resolved to create a new teaching facility at Buhemba, it was entirely funded by a compulsory levy on every member of every parish. The minimum amount stipulated was a thousand shillings, and whilst that only amounts to 40p, when multiplied by 80,000 estimated members it comes to a useful £32,000. In the event, it raised considerably more than that as the more comfortably off members of each parish were expected (and vigorously encouraged) to give more generously. As the emerging middle class continues to grow, so will its members be able to make more realistic contributions to the work of their church. And, as such contributions are compulsory rather than optional, they can become the basis of a planned programme. This may be one idea which it proves difficult to import to Britain, where we prefer to make our own choices about which charity to support rather than obeying the diktat of our bishop, however beloved he may be.

But in Tanzania there is good precedent for such an approach. When I first arrived in Mara in 1989 I was impressed to learn that the villagers had funded the initial work of building a headmaster's house and a laboratory by voluntarily taxing themselves. The way it worked was that for every kilo of cotton sold through the local co-operative, a small percentage was deducted and paid into MEKI, the village education fund. Those who didn't grow cotton could contribute in other ways, after the sale of a cow, goat, sheep, chicken, eggs or other produce. I was chastened to learn later, however, that those who refused to go along with the village council's decision were visited by a team of enforcers who removed anything of value in the culprit's home and sold it at market with the proceeds going to MEKI. I don't think the Bishop of Mara has resorted to such strong arm tactics with his diocesan levy, but the culture of community responsibility in Tanzania is strong.

In other ways, too, a start towards self reliance has been made. Isseco Health Centre, still the only dispensary owned and run by the Church in Mara, has paid its way from day one as far as its running costs are concerned. It has received generous help from parishes in Wakefield, notably Golcar and Battyeford, for its capital development, but its salaries and other running costs are met from that element of school fees which covers medical care and from the modest charges made for the medications it prescribes and then sells. At the same time it is able to deliver free immunisation at its well attended Mother and Child healthcare clinics without running into the red.

The dispensary's parent organisation, Issenye High School, started from scratch and had no alternative but to plan its budget on the basis of 'money in, money out, money left'. The 'money in' came from fees charged to parents, and these had to be in line with what other schools charged, both because of government control and in order to remain competitive. 'Money out' went on staff salaries, books, stationery, food, fuel, and maintenance. 'Money left' was always very little, and the school, like all of Mara's projects, had to be run in a businesslike way. I well remember feeling the shock of this when, moving from a headmaster's office in Kirklees to one in Issenye I abruptly realised that I needed to add accountancy and entrepreneurial skills to those of pedagogy and linguistics I had picked up at university and in the classroom.

Issenye has, of course, received other income over the years, from parishes and schools in Wakefield. They have given generously and this money has been used for capital development expenditure rather than day to day running costs. The school now not only pays its way from the fees charged to parents queuing up to take advantage of the education services it offers, but it also deposits a hefty £9,000 a year into the diocesan CCF, or Church Common Fund.

The Diocese of Mara's Vocational Training Centre (DMVTC) is also self-sufficient in terms of its day to day running costs. As well as purchasing five new computers out of its own resources during the course of my 2013 visit, it was also equipping a new classroom with desks and chairs without any outside help. In addition to being self sufficient, DMVTC already contributes significantly to the CCF and now has plans to build a hostel to accommodate students coming from far away. This will, in true Mara style, both provide a service in response to a demand, and also generate income. There is already a diocesan hostel for general use which charges short or long term visitors modest sums for basic accommodation and also turns a profit. The diocesan Primary School both pays its own way from fees charged to willing parents and produces a surplus in the region of £8,000 annually which goes into the CCF to further bolster diocesan funds. The proposed new secondary school for girls at Bunda will eventually be self sufficient and an income generator. This is surely the way forward.

Three innovative ways of raising money also caught my attention. Adjacent to the centrally located Cathedral at Tarime is a row of rented out lock-up shops, all doing good business and all owned by the diocese, which charges the going rate for rental and makes a healthy profit without incurring any of the commercial risks of running a business. The way in which they raised the capital for this was particularly ingenious. The diocese approached local businessmen who were looking for a well placed location in the busy town and offered them a long lease at favourable rates in return for up-front payment of a year's rent. This enterprise was dreamed up by taking a thoughtful look at the Church's dormant assets, and one of those was land. Throughout all three of Mara's Anglican dioceses there is land not yet being used and Tarime's creative response to that provides a good model for others to copy.

The second enterprise grew on the back of a grant made to Mara's Integrated Community Development Project (ICDP) which included provision for the building of a lecture hall in which to hold seminars. They successfully persuaded the donors to fund the construction of a larger hall than was necessary by offering to hire it out when not in use as a means of generating income and moving towards self reliance. It is now the largest such hall in Musoma town and in regular demand from government and other users ready to pay the going rate.

Perhaps the most enterprising venture I saw, however, was the splendid Rehema project, run by expatriate women living in Musoma who have hit on a way to recycle a little of the surplus income of others like them living in the district. Musoma's European community is made up mainly of church workers of one kind or another from a variety of denominations. They are few in number, but in Tanzanian terms they are relatively well paid. As Musoma is not on any tourist route there are no leisure facilities aimed directly at travellers from developed countries, but Rehema has built a wonderful coffee shop in the Cathedral grounds which, particularly on a Saturday, is full of expatriate families. They meet to relax, exchange news and indulge in such exotic luxuries as bacon sandwiches, cinnamon toast, and skinny lattes. The café is set out under tall shade trees and parents can watch their children share the climbing frame and swings with the occasional vervet monkey hoping for a free lunch. Prices are high, by local standards, reflecting the difficulty of producing such unexpected fare but also in order to fund the project's main purpose.

'Rehema' means mercy in Swahili, and those who benefit from the programme are poor women in Musoma and its environs living in difficult circumstances, perhaps through being widowed with children to raise and no family around, or through illness, disability or impairment of some kind. The café's profits are used to buy material and sewing equipment which is then given to the project's clients, who numbered about a dozen at the time I was there. They then make them into European style dresses and skirts, using patterns supplied, having first been given training in how to do so. They also make small craft objects such as jewellery and reed mats. After passing a strict quality control test these are then bought from the women and later sold in the small shop which is adjacent to the café. A beautiful way of gently soaking the acquiescent rich.

All the initiatives described above raise money. In some cases they simply enable an activity to take place for which there is no other funding available. In others, there is a healthy surplus which helps bankroll those services which will never make money, such as the admirable AIDS ABC Programme. In all of them, profit is not the priority, but the by-product of providing a service for which there is a demand and for which people are willing to pay. I always leave Mara feeling encouraged by such welcome signs of entrepreneurship as a means of delivering the Gospel, and although I hesitate to recommend compulsory collections to the Church of England, I do wonder whether we could not start to consider a few commercially oriented projects.

The admirable Christian African Relief Trust (CART) shows the way. Its second hand shop in Huddersfield takes junk off people's hands, sells it to people for whom it isn't junk, and uses the profit to send a dozen containers a year to Africa. They are stuffed full of discarded goods which would otherwise go to landfill, but which are highly prized there. CART's busy shop in Huddersfield, manned solely by volunteers, has a distinctly 'Mara' look about it.

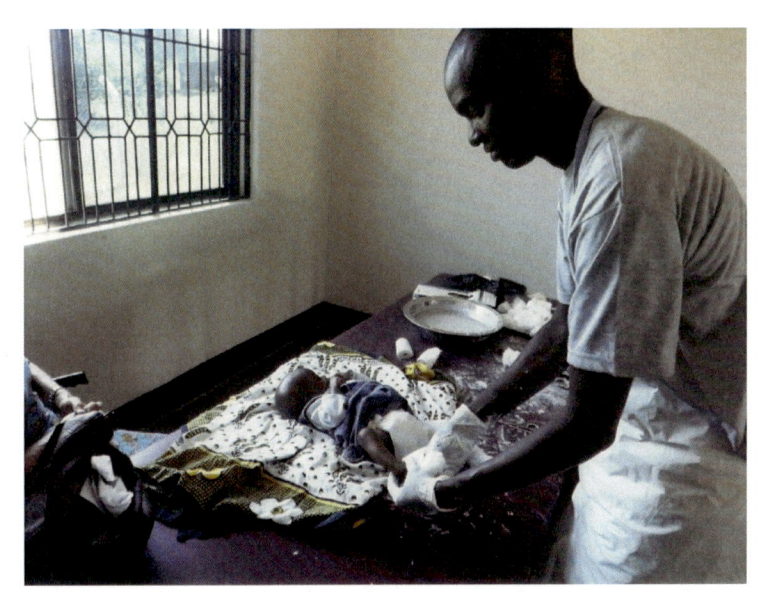

Child with talipes receives treatment at Mara's CBR

Rehema café, Musoma

Chapter 9
Taking charge

One of Mara's more innovative forays into the daily lives of people is its somewhat opaque sounding 'Food Sovereignty and Marketing Project' (FSMP). It aims to improve the livelihoods of rural households in Bunda and Serengeti Districts, which between them cover a vast area in the south of Mara Diocese.

FSMP started in 2012, mounting a pilot phase in three villages within relatively easy reach of its base outside Bunda town. The purpose of this exploratory phase was to see how a new approach called 'Enabling Rural Development' might work in its area of intervention. The key word is 'enabling', as opposed to 'doing'. At the same time, the idea was to equip FSMP staff with the skills to do the job by means of intensive training using outside facilitators. This was followed up with on-the-job experience as they felt their way through the project's pilot stage. The main phase began in January 2013, and was just getting into its stride as I visited Bunda and talked to its manager, Tumaini, a graduate in development studies. She and her marketing officer, Margaret, make a formidable team, with a crystal clear concept of their aims and strategies.

"We target the rural population where almost everyone depends on agriculture for their livelihood," Tumaini said. "The entry points for our intervention are groups of farmers, as in that way we can reach large numbers more effectively and efficiently. We look for a village where we won't be duplicating the efforts of government or other agencies, and where we detect a willingness to work with us. Once we have selected a village we contact the appropriate Local Government Officer and arrange a meeting with him or her in the village and with the people. We work with two farmer groups in each village, so that they can compare notes and learn from each other as well as from us. At those meetings we discuss what they see as their problems and explore ways in which they can get from where they are to where they want to be. We start by looking at what they actually have, and we go on from there."

  That means looking at what they grow, how they grow it, and where they sell it. What animals do they have? Could they introduce different ones? Are they using the best seeds? Is there a market for crops they are not growing now but which they could? It also means identifying the problems they face, such as drought, lack of capital, pests and diseases that affect their crops and animals. Following from that they give advice and information about new varieties of seeds and pesticides, and suggest new outlets for marketing as well as ways of banding together to form a united sellers' market and so avoid being short changed off by more astute and market-savvy buyers.

  The initial survey that Tumaini and Margaret carried out showed that few local farmers had received any form of training for what they did, relying solely on what their forefathers had done for generations past. FSMP's input has already had an invigorating effect on their attitude to the business they are in, and to their output.

"We have already started work with 6 farmer groups," Tumaini said, "and we expect to have reached 40 by the end of 2015. The most important thing we do is to encourage them to make an action plan – something they have never done in the past. This gives them a goal to aim for and offers rewards for reaching it."

Reading the FSMP's own action plan I was surprised to see that, along with agriculture, animal husbandry, business acumen, marketing and self reliance, other elements such as relationships, forgiveness and salvation were listed as subjects for discussion with each group. The programme is as much about how to work together collaboratively and honestly as it is about the nitty-gritty of what to do. It is about how to live, but based on the daily activities of people rather than on their observance of regular worship or adherence to doctrinal belief.

Even more surprising was the revelation that there is no cash involved. The service obviously costs money, as Tumaini and her team are paid employees, but no charge is made for their services. For the moment, they are funded by *Horizont^{3000} Austria* whose philosophy is that, as the people of God, we are called not just to live in the third millennium, but to actively shape it. It is difficult to think of a project which pursues that objective better than FSMP. So far, 150 households have been enrolled and by the end of 2015 the plan is to reach one thousand families who, encouraged by the Church, will be shaping their futures rather than simply living them.

"We are determined not to make ourselves indispensible," Tumaini continued. "We simply open their eyes to the possibilities that exist and encourage them to believe that they can take advantage of them. We want them to take charge of their own lives. And we want them to see that they can do that in ways that don't hurt each other."

Through this structured approach to nudging a whole community into more successful and more caring ways of making a living it is performing the 'Big Society' role with which the Church in Britain was traditionally associated for centuries before our politicians attempted to appropriate it as a way of avoiding their responsibilities. There are churches and church organisations in Britain who do this. The excellent *Christians Against Poverty* organisation works tirelessly to give the sort of advice and encouragement to individuals which Tumaini and her colleagues are delivering to whole communities, but for many churches such activities are seen as the business of the state. At a time when government is withdrawing unapologetically from as much of its social welfare programme as it thinks it can get away with, we have not only an opportunity but a duty to step into the breach, and it could be that Mara is showing us how to do it and reclaim our former rôle.

The challenge for the Church in today's Britain is to adapt a technique that appears to be working well in a rural, agricultural and pastoral society to one where people are in (or sometimes out) of paid employment. The key to that is to exercise the professionalism displayed by FSMP in doing the ground work first.

Find out where people are. Discover where they want to be. Help them see how they might get there.

The newly elected Archbishop of Canterbury's declaration of war on so-called pay-day loan companies is an encouraging sign, and a timely reminder to those outside the Church and those inside it that we are in the business of life – Monday to Saturday as well as that modest proportion of our time in church on a Sunday.

Church Council of Elders in rural parish, Tarime

Teaching in a village setting, Mara

Chapter 10
The Key to Life

A Swahili proverb known throughout Tanzania says that 'Education is the Key to Life' and an associated one that 'Education has no end.' These two beliefs embody the Church in Mara's approach to outreach. Its project workers are typically engaged in programmes addressing health and development issues, but each is designed to educate the people it targets rather than simply to present them with a ready-made solution which they can take off the shelf, use and discard. Time and time again in Mara one comes across the word 'sustainability' and the way in which the Church aims to achieve this is by involving people in the process of education about their needs. This enables them to identify for themselves the resources within their communities which are available to them and which they can activate and develop long after the church programme has ended.

Beneficiaries in the villages say 'The church has shown us how to do this' rather than 'The church did this for us' and there is an evident sense of pride in learning new things as well as gratitude for tangible help in acquiring seeds, a cow, a goat shed or a water tank. The oft-quoted aphorism that it is better to teach someone how to fish than to give them a fish to eat makes even more sense when it comes to setting up a fish farm. Teach someone how to rear fish and they don't even need a rod and line. To illustrate that particular example, the

Church always accompanies such a project with teaching, both formal and informal, about the nutritional value of different food sources and the health benefits that can accrue by adopting a more varied diet than the traditional staples of maize, cassava and sweet potatoes.

The thirst for education in the more narrowly understood sense of the word is universal throughout Tanzania. Parents everywhere want a better life for their children than the one they have had themselves, and in Tanzania they see education as the means of achieving it. Mara is responding to that thirst extraordinarily well. Its nursery, primary, secondary and vocational institutions are all firmly established and widely regarded as centres of excellence with long waiting lists and plans to expand in order to meet an apparently insatiable demand.

Issenye Nursery School

One of the universally recognisable sounds across the globe is that of children at play, so I was surprised when making an unannounced visit to Issenye's Nursery School to hear not a whisper as I approached. Walking in through the open door I saw 51 young children, aged between three and six, working industriously under the supervision of two young women, who greeted me courteously and offered me a seat. Each child had an exercise book and was laboriously making repeated attempts at marking letters and numbers in it, using a pencil. Unusually, the entrance of a pale-skinned stranger caused no great interest and, after a cursory glance in my direction, each child continued to work, head bent closely over the page and tiny fingers forcing the pencil to make the required marks.

The classroom walls were decorated with murals depicting the animals to be found in real life only a few miles away on the Serengeti plain, clearly visible behind them. They had been painted by volunteers from Wakefield and are still in good condition – such a contrast with the grimy walls of most classrooms in Tanzania, where paint is a luxury well down on most people's shopping list.

From time to time, a child took her exercise book up to one of the teachers and stood very close to her for a word of approval and that all important tick alongside the morning's effort. That will be shown with pride to her parents that evening. These are the children of teachers and ancillary staff at the school and they are getting the same sort of jump-start in their educational life that their counterparts in Britain seek, but under wildly differing circumstances. There are no government funded free places here – parents have to pay the modest charges needed to employ staff and provide resources, and they are willing to do so.

ACT Mara Primary School

Tanzanian children join secondary school after completing seven years of primary education, which should start at the age of seven. At the time of independence, all primary schools were in government hands and a massive programme of expansion was undertaken by the new state. The positive side of this was that education was now offered to the masses, rather than to an elite minority. The gratifying result was that Tanzania achieved one of Africa's highest literacy rates, with most people other than the very old able to read, write and do sums. The need for teachers to staff so many new schools, however, led the government to resort to a similar step to that taken by our own educationists in the 19th Century when, under the 'Bell Monitorial System', the ablest pupils were promoted to teacher status after a short period of training.

In Tanzania this led to an inevitable drop in standards from those achieved by more qualified teachers dealing with a fraction of the number of pupils. A major casualty of this was English Language teaching, as large numbers of the newly recruited teachers did not have the necessary skills to teach an ambitious syllabus which was supposed to prepare pupils for English medium secondary school education. The brutal transition from primary schooling in Swahili to secondary education in the English language has had a damping down effect on achievement, and all secondary schools, including Issenye, have been obliged to devise ways of compensating for this with intensive English teaching for the Form I intake.

There is, of course, a point of view that deplores the use of 'colonial' English in Tanzanian schools and there have been frequent calls to use the national language, Swahili, throughout the educational system. Those demands are usually answered by pointing out that such a policy would restrict Tanzanians to texts and other information written in Swahili and would thus disadvantage them in the age of the internet, where

English is undisputed king. This argument is familiar to us in Europe, where small countries such as Holland and Sweden promote the use of English to grant their citizens access to the world of science and technology. One unfortunate result of this for Britons is that we remain firmly monoglot whilst our continental neighbours switch from one language to another with ease. Tanzanians do better than us on that score, and English is usually a third language for them after their native tribal tongue and then Swahili. They are all linguists.

In recent years, a new sort of primary school, privately funded, has emerged and parents have been quick to perceive how much better their pupils have done as they have progressed to secondary level. These new primary schools are using English language in all subjects from the outset so pupils are exposed to it at a much earlier age, when most educationists believe it is easier to learn a fresh language. Mara Diocese took the lead in this movement when it opened its own ACT Mara Primary School in the Millennium Year of 2000.

Thirteen years on and the school is an outstanding success. Its ambitious aim is 'To change society by giving the younger generation a good start and to provide effective leadership for the nation'. Head teacher Appiyah walked me round each class, starting with the tiny five year olds who do two years' nursery school before moving up to Standard I in the Junior section, where they will spend a further seven years. Everything is taught in English and Appiyah says that by Year 3 most pupils can manage to converse in that language. The truth of her claim became apparent as we moved up the years and the answers to my questions became more and more fluent. They had their own questions, too.

"In which part of England do you live?" was one, but that which threw me most was "What year were you born?" The answer (1936 for the record) produced an astonished gasp which proved that, not only had they understood the question and its reply, but also that they were suitably bemused by such an impressive display of longevity.

At the end of seven years all pupils in Tanzania, whether in government or private schools, take the national Standard VII examination. A pass usually ensures entry to a government secondary school and is highly prized as this is the least expensive way to continue in education. Pass rates nationally vary between 30% and 70%, but Appiyah proudly told me that, since opening in 2000, not one pupil had failed this important test.

Such an achievement reflects well on Appiyah and her staff of 15 teachers, all local except for the occasional volunteer from overseas. The conditions under which they work are also key factors in such a remarkable statistic. They are so far removed from what any government school can offer that we might as well be on different planets. Freshly painted classrooms fitted out with neat desks and chairs; a spacious and enclosed playground with shady trees to ward off the sun; a well stocked library and even a new, air-conditioned computer room; all these and a quiet, business-like but happy atmosphere makes ACT Mara a delight to visit.

All this comes at a cost, of course. The basic fee that parents pay is £176 a year. School dinners cost a further £40 a year, and transport in the school's shiny new minibus a further £40. Whilst such modest sums must seem incredibly cheap to anyone in Britain contemplating private education for their children, in Mara they are not inconsiderable. I had assumed that the school largely caters for relatively wealthy Tanzanians, and I have no problem with that. Their children need education and if they are prepared to pay for that, why should the Church not make good provision for them and reap the rewards, which can then be put to use in its ministry to the poor?

Back in her office, though, Appiyah told me that many of her pupils come from modest homes, but that their parents are ready to make sacrifices in order to give them a flying start. Some fail to find the money to renew each year and she is then faced with the delicate business of balancing her books in a caring way. The school, which is located in the Nyamatare suburb of Musoma, has a long standing relationship with the Wakefield parish of Lightcliffe which is linked with Nyamatare, and there have been reciprocal visits, highly valued by those at each end of the link. ACT Mara is clearly thriving and has grown to such an extent that it is now bursting at the seams. Class sizes are unacceptably high, but this is because prospective parents still come to the school begging for places. They are motivated to do so by the school's outstanding record of achievement – top of the league tables for the whole of Mara Region for the last four years.

As with all of Mara's projects, ACT Mara is open to all and, despite its openly Christian ethos it attracts Muslim families as well as Christian. From time to time, some Muslim parents have been pressured into withdrawing their children on the grounds that they should be in an Islamic rather than a Christian school, but many of those who have done so have later returned, pleading to have their children taken back.

There is no room to expand. Every inch of the school's property is now in use, so a new site has been found and three new classrooms were under construction during my visit in early 2013.

Issenye High School

The story of Issenye is told elsewhere* but every time I return I am made vividly aware that what was written then was only the beginning. Now, 23 years after the school was opened it is barely recognisable. The original 90 students have grown to 530, all of them boarders with hostels covering what was bare and stony ground. New and renovated classrooms and staff houses accommodate them, as well as the 23 teachers and 30 non-teaching staff needed to run such a large, 24 hour enterprise.

A powerful generator supplies power from 7pm to 10.30pm, enabling evening studies to take place in unsupervised silence. Solar panels supplement this source of power whilst waiting for an eventual hook-up to the national grid. Water is on tap, pumped up to school by

School for the Serengeti, published 2007

solar power from a deep well. New water tanks also harvest rainwater directed into them from classroom and dormitory roofs and the daily trips to the spring are a thing of the past.

Work has started on a new kitchen adjoining the huge multi-purpose dining hall and the recent installation of a biogas unit has transformed cooking facilities. For those whose image of a school in Africa is a group of children squatting in the shade of a tree learning how to read and write, Issenye High School will undoubtedly disappoint. It is even identified on Google Earth.

The school's academic record is good. In the national league tables Issenye is always first among the 23 secondary schools of Serengeti District, and always in the top 10% across the country. The first student to register at Issenye in 1990 was called George. He was also the first to turn up for lessons after every holiday during his four years there. Not only that, he was invariably first in most of the examinations he sat there. By rights, he should have gone to a government secondary school rather than fee-paying Issenye, but his Christian father declined to pay the necessary bribe, so he was refused admission. After the death of his father, George was without the means to continue with his education, but was fortunate enough to attract funding from individuals in Wakefield Diocese. They saw him through his years at Issenye, and then through his 'A' levels at High School, and his subsequent career at university. All this took time, with breaks in between to earn enough money to keep body and soul together. Just thirteen years after registering as 'Number 1' at Issenye, he became its first university graduate.

George is unusually bright and is one of the young Tanzanians who will eventually help his country pull itself up by its own bootstraps with his specialist skills (in mechanical engineering) and his wholehearted dedication to Christian values and hard work. Without the opportunities offered to him by the Diocesan Secondary School at Issenye, he would be just another hard working subsistence farmer making ends meet in the good times and going hungry in the bad. He is a shining example of the motto at the head of this chapter and it was a great day in 2010 when he made a return visit to Issenye and addressed the assembled students with a motivational talk about getting on with their studies.

At a February 2013 meeting of Serengeti District's 23 secondary schools, Issenye's current head, Joseph Nyamgoncho, was asked for the secret of his success. He pointed first to the practice of beginning each day with prayer and the school's insistence on moral behaviour based on Christian values. He then told them that teachers stay at Issenye for a long time, thus providing continuity. He himself is the best example of that, having been there for twenty years.

There is no complacency at Issenye, however. In common with all Tanzania's secondary schools, examination results in 2012 were worse than expected. As this was an across-the-board phenomenon it is widely accepted that something went wrong with the marking mechanism. It is improbable that a whole cohort of students should be less able than their predecessors.

At a staff meeting I attended, however, teachers made plans to improve the motivation and performance of both teachers and students so as to achieve better results next time. At a subsequent meeting of teachers and students it was agreed, without demur, to have extra lessons after normal school hours. I struggle to imagine this happening in Britain.

Not all children are as academically gifted as George, but Issenye has brought out the best in them equally well, though in different ways. Another boy who started at Issenye in its first year and in the same class as George was called Mgendi. His family were reluctant to let him come, seeing no need for a 'scholar' in their midst. Mgendi was desperate to learn, however, and independently funded his studies by providing milk for the school from his own cow. Unlike George, he struggled academically and made a poor showing in his final examinations. His whole attitude to school and to life, however, showed that he had untapped potential which, allied to his boundless enthusiasm for hard work, led to his appointment as Projects Officer when he had completed his four years at the school. He learned to drive, to keep simple accounts, to manage the school shop, camp site, grinding mill and café, and to fix leaking gutters, entertain tourists, repair water tanks, change tyres, paint walls and do the myriad other tasks needed to keep a place like Issenye going. He eventually enrolled at a school for motor vehicle maintenance in Arusha, and became a competent mechanic as well.

He proved to be unusually resourceful and is one of the young Tanzanians who have demonstrated to an approving rural community that education can, indeed, change your life, and change that of people around you. Without the opportunities offered him by Issenye Secondary School, he would be just another cow man, looking after his father's herds, and then inheriting them, with little vision of what else life might have in store for him.

Private schools such as Issenye receive no subsidy from the government so have to charge fees in order to pay salaries and provide books, equipment, accommodation and food. Full boarding costs at Issenye range between £300 and £400 per annum depending on the year group. To put such a sum in perspective, a graduate teacher earns about that each month, so it is a manageable, but not a trifling, sum.

Those parents who wish to educate their children privately but who are not on a comfortable salary have to find the money in some other way. Wealth is often accumulated on the hoof rather than in a bank. The 2013 price of a cow is £120/£200 and it can always be converted into cash when the need arises. Haven't got a cow? Tanzanians know how to start small, hence the successful fundraising effort during Issenye's early days which invited sponsors to emulate parents by helping children 'go to school on an egg'. Eggs produce chickens, which can be traded up to a sheep, then a goat and eventually a cow via a recognised and universally accepted exchange rate.

When Issenye was a day school we pegged fees at the price of one cow. Occasionally parents would bring us an actual cow, but such animals often proved to have a bad limp or a troublesome cough so we began to insist that their owners should sell the cow first then bring us the cash. The present fees are the equivalent of two cows, but the school is now fully boarding, with all food and accommodation costs included.

Joseph welcomed me to the greatly extended guest house which now boasts nine double bedrooms, many of them ensuite. Despite being whimsically known as the Savoy, facilities are still simple – a shower involves upending a jug of water over the head, but it is hot water prepared before daylight by Susanna, a teacher's wife employed when necessary to look after the many visitors. She is seldom without work. On my most recent visit I shared the accommodation with government-appointed supervisors and two soldiers, at Issenye to oversee the Form VI examinations then taking place. At other times, groups of parishioners, teachers and students from Wakefield Diocese stay there, helping out at school and learning about life in a culture markedly different from their own. Their regular visits stimulate students and staff alike and are one of the many factors that differentiate Issenye from other schools in Mara. I arrived on this latest visit full of expectation as what I might see.

Joseph first took me to morning assembly and positioned me before the ranks of frankly curious students in their smart, proudly worn uniforms. He gave them an extended history of the school, which was opened before any of them were born and produced me as though from a dusty cupboard unopened for two decades. How implausibly old we both must seem to these eager young people setting out at the very beginning of their adult lives.

Assembly over, the students quietly dispersed to their classrooms. The school was in the middle of examinations. Though privately owned and funded, Issenye is fully integrated into the state system, following the national curriculum, submitting itself to governmental inspection and taking state examinations at 'O' and 'A' level. This morning's was practical chemistry. In many schools this would be what is referred to as a 'theoretical practical' with beakers and flasks drawn on the board, then verbal and written explanations of what would be done with them if they were real. Not so at Issenye with its well-equipped laboratory. Everything was ready for them and the confident sixth formers stepped inside to repeat the experiments they had made over the year. Elsewhere, classes in English language, religious education, mathematics, history, geography, Swahili, physics, chemistry, biology and civics were in full swing as the school settled down to its normal routine.

The *askari* on duty outside the laboratory where the examination was taking place gave me a friendly wave and adjusted his rifle to settle more comfortably across his shoulder. In many parts of the country there have been sporadic scandals over the years with question papers appearing on sale in advance of the exam, surrogate candidates taking examinations and answers being retrospectively filled in. The government's heavily over-the-top response has been to send in the army and so Issenye, as every other secondary school, now had two soldiers stationed on campus for the duration.

The early morning rain had stopped and the sun swiftly dried out the ground and burned off the last remnant of cloud, leaving only a deep blue bowl of sky above. The welcome rain was no more than a disappointing shower.

"I'll show you some real water now," Joseph said. We made our way through ranks of pink flowering frangipani trees to the highest point of the school campus, behind the girls' hostels and looking out over the vast expanse of the Serengeti – the 'endless plain' in the Maasai language. As we approached a pair of 5,000 litre poly-tanks mounted on a concrete platform we could hear water constantly trickling into them. We walked round to the other side and saw the outlet pipe, plunging into the ground on its way down to school. We followed a rough path through the teachers' *shambas*, now filled with ripening maize and green leaved cassava plants. This path marks the route of the inlet pipe, and the water was making its way to school in the opposite direction to the one we were taking. We walked steadily downhill for a quarter of a mile, then came across a sturdy metal frame on which rested a bank of 85w solar panels. They power a pump which constantly lifts the water from a capped well encased in concrete. The flow is modest, but continuous, at least during those times when the sun is shining – and at Issenye that means most daylight hours.

The 86m deep well replaces the old one which was less than half as deep and was prone to seasonal variation. This one had only been in use for a month, but the technicians who installed it are confident that it will never run dry. It is also 'good water', free of salt or any other contamination. The only problem with it will be if a prolonged spell of cloudy weather prevents the solar panels from lifting the water to the school. But then, clouds mean rain and the school is continuing to sink underground storage tanks next to its large roofs in order to harvest rainwater. Belt and braces make good sense.

"Now we'll look at the biogas system," Joseph said, with evident pride. "It's all part of the same project." He told me that the total cost of the combined water and biogas installation was a staggering £33,000 and I asked him how he was able to find such a sum.

"It's a gift from VIP," he said. VIP is a high-end Safari Lodge not too far from school which caters for wealthy tourists, mostly American, who want to see the Serengeti in style and who are reputedly prepared to pay up to a thousand dollars a day for the privilege. It is owned by a Mr Jones, sadly unrelated, whose family name is incorporated in the New York based Dow-Jones share index. The VIP hotel chain evidently has money to spare and is investing similar sums in institutions around the national park as a contribution to the local economy. Such an apparently benevolent policy also draws some of the sting out of accusations that it is exploiting Tanzania's assets and siphoning off the profits for the benefit of overseas share-holders, but locally it is seen as a benefactor, and a major employer of cooks, maids, drivers, guides, managers and other staff.

Joseph attracted their interest by talking to a team of technicians who were installing a water tank at nearby Natta. He invited them to come and look at the school and when they came, they liked what they saw and suggested that a combined water and biogas scheme would be the most beneficial programme.

We walked back up to school and went into the new kitchen being installed at one end of the enormous dining room, which is now Mara Region's biggest roofed building. The biogas unit was being tried out for the first time and as the tap was turned on, we all looked hopefully at the large boiler – one of five being installed. Today it had only water in it for this test run, but when in full operation it will produce *ugali* in the sort of quantity needed for 600 students and staff. Before long the water started to bubble and then clouds of steam rose from its surface and we raised a ragged cheer and took photographs. It's another significant milestone in the school's development.

"So where does the gas actually come from?" I asked. Joseph took me outside again and we stood on a large area of disturbed soil beneath which he said there is a large chamber 'as big as a house'.

"That's where all the toilet outlets now go," he said. There is also an inlet for adding cattle dung, which will combine with human waste to make the mixture more suitable for the production of biogas. It is the perfect solution to two problems - disposal of sewage and production of fuel. And there are two hidden bonuses. Firstly, using biogas in the school kitchen will greatly reduce the amount of daily firewood consumed, and thus have less impact on the environment. Secondly, when the human and cattle detritus has yielded its precious fuel, the residue makes an inoffensive compost which will fertilise the school's kitchen garden. The garden will consequently produce more food, which will be fed to the school community, whose members will obligingly process it in the usual way, thus producing more biogas and more residue which will then…..

It's a closed system of almost poetic symmetry. I congratulated Joseph on his success in attracting such a generous and technically informed benefactor, then we reminisced on how far the school has come since those days more than twenty years ago when we were struggling to develop the school virtually one brick at a time. It's a classic case of success breeding success. The school's steady climb up district, regional and national league tables has attracted the attention of parents, politicians, ministers and now such organisations as VIP who all want to be associated with it.

The village and the Anglican Church, working co-operatively, are now reaping the harvest of their early ploughing and sowing. That harvest is the number of young men and women who have passed through the classrooms of Issenye since 1990 and are now helping to build the new Tanzania. Issenye graduates are scattered across the country in significant numbers doing worthwhile jobs that add value to the country as a whole as well as improving their own lives and that of their families. They also take with them core Christian values based on their years in a caring environment with ethical values and strong discipline. There is currently a move to establish an association of alumni who will be expected to help others follow in their footsteps. In the Age of Facebook and Twitter, it might even happen.

Mara Vocational Training Centre

When I first visited The Diocese of Mara's Vocational Training Centre (DMVTC) in 1989 it was located in a grim, rented building on a side street in Musoma town centre. The outside walls were of crumbling mud. Those inside were roughly plastered but were unpainted. Three rooms each held rickety desks at which were seated immaculately clean and well dressed young men and women, who rose respectfully to their feet as I was ushered in. They were learning English language, book keeping, typing and sewing. Resources were scarce and amounted to a few battered typewriters and discarded sewing machines which would have looked more at home in a museum. Their teachers were working hard in challenging circumstances and the resulting atmosphere was one of optimism and endeavour.

Twenty-four years on and that same atmosphere now exists at DMVTC's new building close to Mara's St John's Cathedral. Shady trees make for a pleasant environment and I approached with keen anticipation. The head teacher stepped out to greet me and I saw that it was Nyabasi, a former student at Issenye. She is now an accomplished educator who went on from her secondary studies to gain a teaching diploma. It was particularly pleasing to see her in such a high profile job as she came from the simplest of backgrounds in one of Issenye's five villages. We caught up on old times and then she proudly escorted me round the newly built classrooms, freshly painted and full of eager young men and women bent on improving their lives through education. In common with other diocesan projects, the aim of DMVTC is to provide unconditional service to the community - 'To become a centre of excellence for vocational education and training in Mara Region and in Tanzania at large,' in the words of its brochure. Nyabasi says that whereas in years gone by most applicants were those who failed to go to secondary school, many are now Form IV leavers who recognise that adding vocational skills to their academic achievements will make them more employable in the increasingly dynamic society that is the new Tanzania. The courses offered are not markedly different from those of twenty-four years ago, but now there are more than a hundred students, and they study to a higher level.

The sewing classes have been handed over to the Mothers' Union. This is not as sexist as it may sound to European ears as sewing is traditionally a male preserve in Tanzania, perhaps because it involves a machine, but these young women are changing all that.

Typing, now discarded in Britain in favour of word processing, is still taught because many organisations in Tanzania still employ typists.

"But won't that die out?" I asked Nyabasi.

"Yes," she replied, "but their typing skills are then easily transferable to word processing. Now come and have a look next door." We entered another room which was full of computers. Many would be considered obsolete in Britain, but they are fully functional and many had two students in front of them, helping each other in typical Tanzanian co-operative learning style. Muslim girls sat alongside their Christian fellow students and were content to be photographed. The college accepts applicants from whatever background. They were overseen by Rose, another product of Issenye and headmaster Joseph's daughter. She, too, greeted me warmly and continued her supervision of her class, who were all fully absorbed in mastering the complexities of Word™, Publisher™ and Excel.™ Nyabasi pointed out the antiquity of the computers.

"I now have one hundred students, all wanting to learn computer skills," she said, "but we just don't have enough machines." The winding up of the excellent 'Faith in Action' organisation has been a severe blow to Mara. The annual delivery of a container full of discarded computers, typewriters, duplicators, bed sheets, bandages, blankets, curtains, baby packs, clothing, shoes, stationery, exercise books, pens, pencils, sewing materials, soap and a thousand other items, all freely given, came to an abrupt halt when the cost of transport exceeded the ability of the organisers to raise the funds needed to pay it.

The good news, however, is that serviceable computers are now available in Musoma, brand new, for about £190. Nyabasi said that five were now on order and would be installed next week. She explained that DMVTC is already fully self-supporting as far as revenue is concerned. That is, she can pay her staff wages and other running costs out of the fees paid by students, but that for capital investment she has so far had to rely on outside help. In this instance, however, she has managed to conserve sufficient money to make a major investment. It's a good sign. The 'computer only' courses are concentrated, lasting for only four weeks, and so more easily affordable and correspondingly very popular.

An average 45 students attend at any one time, which means that between five and six hundred a year are being taught these vital skills.

Longer courses are available which teach English language, typing, office practice, secretarial duties and computer skills under the umbrella of NABE, the National Business Examinations organisation. NABE qualifications are much sought after across Tanzania and Nyabasi's young charges are making themselves highly employable. Nyabasi was excited about the imminent arrival of a shorthand teacher. No shorthand training exists in Mara so far, she thinks, and she knows that this will attract more students.

Bunda Girls' School

The battle for top of the secondary league tables in Mara Region is always between Issenye, Makoko and Kowak Girls' School. The latter two are both long established and run by the Roman Catholic Church, with financial aid from America. The rising demand for girls' education is itself a sign of development within Tanzania, and one to which the Anglican Church is responding. Numbers of girl entrants at Issenye have always been high but, as in Britain, there is mounting evidence that girls do better when they are not learning alongside boys.

Mara Diocese now has a plan to emulate the success of both Issenye and Kowak Girls' School by establishing its own 'girls only' secondary school at Bunda. It's a shrewd move which achieves the twin aim of responding to a need within the community and also providing a further income stream for the diocese and thereby increasing its march towards self reliance.

Education *is* the key to life, but as we know so well in Britain, it does not come value-free. It is perfectly possible to be well educated but devoid of any 'moral compass'. Mara Diocese has indelibly stamped its name and its values on formal education in this part of Tanzania, and rather than resting on its laurels is still looking to expand. The future of Tanzania is in the hands of young Tanzanians and the thought of so many young people being educated within the Church's caring ethos of service and love is reassuring. If it was doing nothing else by way of outreach this would, in itself, be wholly admirable.

ACT Mara Primary class

IT lesson, DMVTC

Issenye's water tanks dwarfing headmaster Joseph

Chapter 11
The generation game

There are worse places to be old than in Mara. On a visit to a parish near Tarime an elderly man approached me. He was bearded and bald, so apart from the trivial issue of skin colour we could have been twins. He glared at me fiercely.

"How old are you?" he barked. I told him. He looked gratified and, looking round at his companions for approval, loudly proclaimed that he was two years older than me. The group of parishioners plainly felt uncomfortable that a guest from overseas had been so comprehensively bested in this confrontation, and they moved quickly to put things right. They did so by making conciliatory noises and assuring me that, even though I may actually be younger than my inquisitor, I did look considerably older. I did my best to look pleased about this. I had already got used to being addressed as *Mzee*, which translates as 'old man' and accepting that it is a deferential form of address. Whilst acceptable in Swahili, however, I have found myself bristling at being so addressed in English. We have gone so far down the 'youth culture' road in Britain that having attention drawn to the passage of time is rarely welcome until we get into our nineties and can start bragging about it.

In such a context it is difficult to imagine anyone in Britain choosing a nickname defining themselves as a grandparent in the hope of attracting customers, but that is what Ambilikili Mwasapile did in Loliondo District, across the Serengeti from Mara. Known as *'Babu'* (Granddad) he started selling a concoction he called *mugariga* that he claimed would cure AIDS and other major ailments, including diabetes, hypertension, and epilepsy. It didn't, of course, but his personal history as a retired Lutheran pastor and his sanctified status as *Babu* gave him a respectability and credibility that led to thousands flocking to his remote village from across Tanzania, Kenya and Uganda for his 'miracle cure'.

Catastrophically, many patients stopped taking their anti-retroviral medication after making the trek to his village, several hours away from any decent road. Lines of four wheel drive vehicles and minibuses crawled along, stretching for miles as people, often very ill, tried to reach him. Some of the more wealthy avoided the trek by flying in on helicopters. His visitors included prominent government officials such as Tanzania's deputy minister for Water and Irrigation. *Babu* even had a Facebook page, where people from as far away as Romania reached out to him for help.

Age is respected in Mara, and the opinions of older people are listened to with serious attention, even when minds have become clouded by the passage of the years. The extended family means that care of the aged is a simpler matter than it is in Britain. Care homes are, for the moment, unknown and surrendering one's parents to an institution is an alien concept which it would be difficult to sell. It is inconceivable that one should not live within a flexible family grouping which can easily accommodate those no longer able to care for themselves.

To achieve this, however, there must be a guaranteed supply of carers, and that means big families. Few things disturb a Tanzanian more than the prospect of growing old with no children around. Without state provision for the elderly, a family has to look after its own. High infant mortality rates and limited access to medical care mean that large families are still the norm. Family planning campaigns can only succeed when parents are sure that their children will survive.

One unlooked-for consequence of increasing education could be that, as high-flying sons and daughters migrate to Dar-es-Salaam, Nairobi, London and New York in pursuit of their careers, they will no longer be able to maintain their present level of support for the elderly. At present, they send money back to the village and it is spread about among other members of the still extended family to help them fulfil their duties. One or two educated visitors to Wakefield from Mara, however, have expressed great interest in our residential care homes for the elderly, and requested a visit. They have left looking very thoughtful.

Whilst the encounters related above may seem to give elders all the cards in Mara, the respect which the young give to the old has its own obligations. Strolling through the streets of Musoma I overtook two small children.

"*Shikamoo*," they greeted me, the appropriate way to address someone significantly older than oneself. It literally means "I grasp your feet," with the attendant implication that you will then kiss them. I offered the equally obligatory *"Marahaba,"* which means "Delightful!" Had I not done so I would have been condemned as a social outcast by anyone witnessing the exchange. Indeed I was once pursued by an angry and embarrassingly articulate mother whose infant child strapped to her back had apparently addressed me with a whispered '*shikamoo*' to which I had unwittingly, but unforgivably, failed to respond.

Such exchanges are essential to the social structure of Tanzania. Respect for age and experience is universal, but acknowledgement of that respect is as important as its rendition. My two young companions and I paused to continue our conversation. They were mesmerised by my hairy arms, unknown in Africa except on monkeys, but they were far too polite to make any such comparison out loud. I learned that they were on their way home from school, which I could have guessed from their immaculate miniature uniforms.

"What did you learn at school today?" I asked, rather unimaginatively. They told me they had been doing sums.

"Do you like school?" I asked.

"Oh yes," they replied. "We like it very much."

"And how old are you?" I continued.

"I'm four, but he's only three," the confident little girl answered, suitably scornful of her impossibly juvenile companion. We continued to exchange information for a while and then said appropriate goodbyes and went on our separate ways. I watched them successfully navigate their passage through crowds of adult pedestrians, speeding motorbikes, over-laden wheelbarrows and the occasional car bumping its way over Musoma's ubiquitous potholes.

They felt, and were, perfectly safe in this urban environment and I thought back to the convoys of cars that deposit our children, one at a time, at school every morning and collect them each evening to save them the strenuous exercise of walking, and also to protect them from the imagined horrors which might befall them outside the safety of home and school.

I remembered Mahatma Gandhi when, on his first trip outside India, he was asked by an incautious newspaper reporter:

"What do you think of European civilisation, Mr Gandhi?"

"I think it would be a very good idea," he replied.

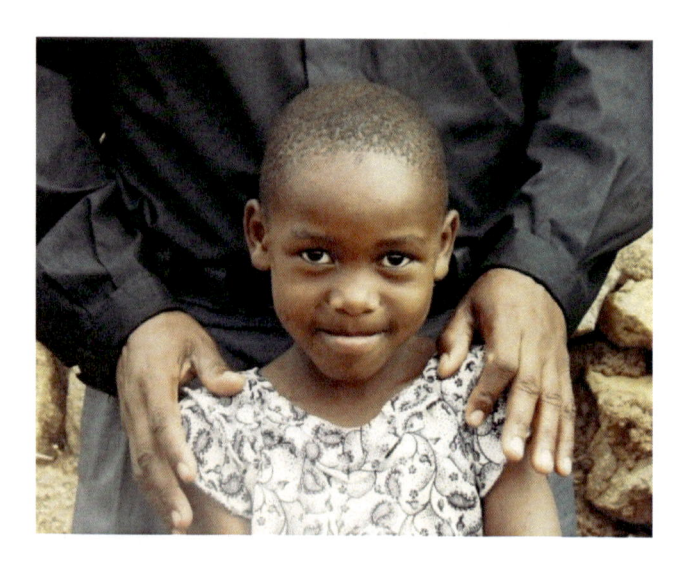

In safe hands

Chapter 12
Buhemba

Buhemba, in the Butiama District of Mara, is the oldest of its projects, pre-dating the creation of the diocese itself. It covers an area of 1,000 acres and lies 30 miles, or an hour and a half hour's drive away from Musoma, unless it has been raining heavily, in which case it takes much longer over the sticky mud roads. Buhemba was originally established in 1965 as a commercial farm designed to create food and to create an income for the Church through the sale of its produce. The site was chosen for its inherent fertility and the change in soil structure is clearly visible as you approach.

A secondary aim was to provide development services to the whole of Lake Zone – a vast area which includes Mara, Shinyanga, Mwanza and Kagera Regions. It was this aspiration which encouraged Julius Nyerere to help the Church acquire the land from local Zanaki people.

Australian missionaries supervised the building of barns, grain silos, and solid houses with water tanks, flush lavatories and plumbing. They imported heavy agricultural machinery and worked the land on a grand scale for many years. By the mid nineteen eighties, however, the project had lost its momentum. Much of the machinery lay rusting in the barns and there was only a vestigial amount of farming activity. Other uses were made of the buildings; some were rented out to workers at the nearby gold mine in Maji Moto, but as 'Buhemba Rural Aid Centre' (BRAC) it was barely functional.

In 1993, however, BRAC was re-invented as 'Buhemba Rural *Agricultural* Centre', with a subsidiary organisation known as Buhemba Farm Services, BFS. The deliberate dropping of 'Aid', with its potentially patronising overtones of dishing out help, carried with it a philosophy of participation and co-operation with the local community that is now apparent at every level of a reinvigorated Buhemba and in the entire diocese.

In the twenty years since the rebranding of BRAC it has changed. The well constructed office block is still there, with its neatly laid out paths with concrete edges and bright bougainvillea hedges to greet the visitor. Trees offering shade and a variety of fruits dot the entire complex, with almost every one of them proclaiming that they were planted by some distinguished visitor. The staff houses are still in place, along with the cavernous barn-like structures used to shelter the project's vehicles. There are new buildings as well, notably the impressive lecture room and office suite built for the centre's latest initiative, Buhemba Community Training and Development Institute, BCTDI. Even more impressive than the structure itself is the way in which this was funded – entirely from 'voluntary' giving as the result of one of the Bishop's levies described previously. This seemed very much like a 'coming of age' event, with Mara Diocese rejoicing in its emerging ability to fund development without recourse to outside help.

Sitting in the office of the BRAC manager Ezekiel, and looking round whilst he answered the phone, I saw Mother Teresa's dictum pinned to the wall. *"We feel that what we are doing is just a drop in the ocean but oceans would be less because of that missing drop",* it said. Perhaps a little hackneyed to our jaded ears, but when I think of the catalogue of difficulties faced by a poor country whose people largely rely on small scale agriculture to survive, I can sympathise. Mara is huge, and the extent to which the Anglican Church can tackle its multiple problems is severely limited, but its leaders and workers never seem daunted by that. Like Mother Teresa, they just get on with it. Over the next few days I was to see what an ambitious 'drop in the ocean' Buhemba now represents.

Following a survey of the local community it emerged that food insecurity was the main issue for local people, so the diocese set out to establish a programme which aims to eradicate, or at least reduce this. Agriculture, livestock, environmental concerns, water and marketing were identified as the means of implementing such a programme, and they began working with nine villages close by. This has now been expanded to include a further twelve villages, some up to twenty-two miles away. BRAC is now reaching a potential population of 96,840 and is already in active co-operation with 4,800 households comprising some 27,000 individuals.

The approach is through farmer-to-farmer extension methods, with three 'Farmer Motivators' in each village and one or two community based animal health workers. The centre itself provides training in agricultural and livestock issues. Villagers who complete this course are then encouraged to pass on their skills and so become trainers themselves and spread knowledge more widely over the surrounding area. They do all this on a voluntary basis, receiving no payment but encouraged by the gift of a bicycle to help them get around, and a supply of technical literature to improve their knowledge. BRAC's hope is that this method will encourage sustainable development, with 'ownership' handed over to the community and the need for its input gradually fading away.

Diversification is encouraged by the introduction of new crops and new ideas. Cooking oil is in great demand throughout the region It has traditionally come from animal sources in Tanzania, but the climate is ideal for the production of sunflower seeds, which make good quality oil, rich in poly-unsaturated fatty acid and a good source of Vitamin E and folic acid. It is popular, and sells well on Musoma market. A few acres at Buhemba are devoted to sunflower production, mainly as a demonstration plot to show local farmers that it is a practical proposition, for although it is grown in other parts of Tanzania, in Mara it is still a relatively new crop.

A number of BRAC's client villages have now begun to grow the crop and BRAC buys their seed from them, enabling them to cash in on their efforts immediately and on the spot – no trip to Musoma needed. Seeds from this source and from Buhemba farm itself are then processed at the centre and turned into high grade cooking oil, packaged and labelled before sending to Musoma for sale at £6.50 for a five litre container.

Another innovative approach to exploiting readily available plants in order to make a marketable product is in the processing of Jatropha seeds. The Jatropha plant grows as a weed in Tanzania, and can survive in poor soil and in near drought conditions. It has been hailed as a possible source of bio-fuel in other parts of the world, which would be a good thing as it is not edible and would not compete with food crops. Tanzania's neighbour, Mozambique, invested in huge plantations of Jatropha covering tens of thousands of acres and the country's president went from village to village, telling people to plant Jatropha trees. Sadly, that bubble has burst as it turns out that although Jatropha can, indeed, survive drought and poor soil conditions, it does not produce many seeds in those circumstances, so is not suitable for large scale farming production.

The oil in the seeds can also be made into soap, however, and in Mara that is what they do, but on a small scale. I was taken to the village of Kibubwa, where BRAC has installed a hand operated oil press and people collect the seeds from the surrounding areas where it occurs naturally. The seeds are crushed, the oil extracted, and then turned into soap in a simple mould. The residue is used as cattle feed and as manure, so three useful by-products are made. The soap is much sought after and the income derived from this project is making a difference to the local economy. It is so successful that the village has asked the Church to help them buy another machine so as to increase production. In line with its policy of encouraging sustainable self reliance, however, the request was refused. They were advised to re-invest some of their profits in expanding the business, and so learn the complications of doing business in the real world.

We were about to leave the project when a young girl approached carrying a basket on her head. It was full of Jatropha seeds which she was bringing to sell. She had collected them from round about her home and was looking forward to getting a good price for this windfall crop.

"What will you do with the money?" I asked her, thinking that it would doubtless go straight into the family pot rather than be spent on sweets as would most probably have happened in Britain. But no – she had parental permission to spend her earnings on something quite different.

"I will buy exercise books," she said. No school in Tanzania supplies such things and they are a prized acquisition.

Back at the centre I was shown the prototypes of the zero grazing cow and goat enclosures which are now in operation all over Mara. Each was full of healthy looking animals serving as a livestock bank for local villagers. Groups of smallholder farmers are brought here on short courses where they are accommodated, fed and watered, so it seems like a bit of a holiday. In between times they are taught these new methods of farming which result in better crops, higher milk yields and increased understanding of the economics of land management and animal husbandry.

The manager of the farm section at Buhemba (BFS) is retired army officer Lazaro, who told me that his aim is to grow food and sell it. He has also launched a seed production and multiplication programme. The resulting seeds are sold to dealers in Musoma for profit, as are the sunflower seeds, which go to BRAC. The sunflower oil enterprise has proved so successful that Lazaro can't supply all its needs, so he now plans to grow more plants and avoid having to import them from other regions.

BFS also has an educative role, and I saw how the acreage was being increased by use of ox-drawn ploughs. Too often, the belief is that you can only cultivate a large area if you have a tractor, but tractors cost money, use expensive fuel, need maintaining and break down. The 'intermediate technology' of ploughing with oxen has been scorned by politicians, understandably anxious to catapult the country into the modern era, but it has many advantages for poor farmers unable to make the considerable investment needed for mechanisation. They know about cattle and the training they get at Buhemba enables them to rise above the very finite limit of how much ground can be cleared using the heavy *jembe*, or hoe, used for cultivation by hand.

Lazaro's real pride is in his breeding herd of cattle. We walked down to see them along a leafy lane that could have been in rural England on a really hot day with its overhanging trees and grassy banks. Standing patiently in a large enclosure were a number of cattle of obviously mixed parentage, ranging from pure local *Zebu* to three quarters Hereford. In between were F1, F2 and F3 crosses. As the numbers go up, so does the potential milk yield, but the remaining *Zebu* qualities ensure greater tolerance of local conditions and make survival more likely. These 'modern cows' are much sought after by local farmers because of the vastly increased amount of milk, and eventually beef, that they yield. Along with the zero grazing techniques and programme of returning calves to the centre for later passing on to someone else, they have made great differences to many people's lives. The strains are kept to a standard quality by the use of artificial insemination in collaboration with the government laboratory based in Mwanza. This practice may be less than popular with Buhemba's bulls, especially when they learn that their fate is either to be eaten or to be castrated and so converted into the oxen described above.

Other expertise is also taught at Buhemba – all aimed at improving the prosperity and health of its customers. Many local farmers have neglected to put their cattle through the government dipping stations for one reason or another. In some cases the facility has been too far away to make it a practical proposition. Buhemba has resolved this by introducing portable sprayers carried on a back pack which can easily be taken to where the cattle are. Dipping, or spraying, is essential in this part of the world as the ever present East African Tick Disease is a constant threat which leads to the death of an estimated 1.1 million animals a year throughout the region.

New strains of cassava and sweet potato have also been introduced at Buhemba and visiting farmers are encouraged to try them out on their own land by giving them free supplies of seeds or cuttings. These new varieties are resistant to a disease which affects crops all over Tanzania as well as having improved vitamin content, and have been developed at the government's Mwanza facility.

Fish farming and bee-keeping are other innovations which are actively promoted at Buhemba and whilst I was there I saw improved forms of beehives being made by staff for local use. They have even introduced a strain of stingless bees which are proving very popular as African bees are far less docile than their European cousins and are easily provoked into attacking the unwary. Sitting in Ezekiel's office again I listened to his philosophical approach to what Buhemba is about.

"Our core values," he said "are prayer, transparency, co-operation, professionalism, dignity, equity, accountability and sustainability. Our aim is to improve the lives of the smallholders in our area and the wider community by increasing their knowledge, and improving their skills, both in agriculture and animal husbandry as well as in management. The first thing we do is to sit down and listen to them so that we can assess their needs."

"What about evangelism?" I asked.

"We make no attempt to evangelise," he said, "as we don't want to alienate any of our target clientele. We do always start our meetings with prayer, however. Everyone knows we are a church organisation and it would seem strange to do otherwise." He paused, reflecting for a moment and then continued.

"And we have just opened two new parishes in the area. The people just kept asking us to do so, and the Bishop agreed." No words....but then *The Word*.

Jatropha seeds for exercise books

Sunflower oil, Buhemba

Chapter 13
Offshoots

The splitting of the original Mara Diocese did not go easily, or even according to plan. The original concept of having two new entities, one north, the other south, foundered on tribal sensitivities. The small town of Kowak, now in Rorya, is the acknowledged heartland of Christian Mara. It was to here that a certain Archdeacon Owen came south from Kenya to plant the first Anglican church some eighty years ago. At a 1990 jubilee celebration to mark that event there were octogenarian Christians present who remembered it, and it is a sobering thought to realise how young a Church it still is.

Kowak, and the whole of Rorya District in the north-west of Mara, is almost exclusively the home of Luo people, who also occupy a large area of Kenya, to the north. When the suggestion was put that Kowak would be the focus of a new, northern diocese, however, the Kuria people, based in Tarime in the north-east, felt themselves to be unrepresented. They had already built a large, cathedral-sized church in Tarime town and had long hoped that it would be at the centre of any new, northern diocese.

These differences ultimately proved to be insoluble and the result was that a still large Diocese of 'New' Mara, in the south, is now balanced by two relatively small new entities to the north, Luo Rorya and Kuria Tarime. *(See map, Page 8)* Mara itself is far more tribally diverse, with Luo, Kuria, Sukuma, Mjita, Issenye, Zanaki and others living and working side by side. Three years after the split, the two northern dioceses are still working to establish a separate identities.

Rorya, in particular, feels to be out on a limb and bereft of all the projects and services which previously originated in Musoma. I was made very welcome at Kowak by Bishop John Adiema and his recently appointed Link Officer, Peter Oyoo – yet another product of Issenye. I learned that many of Rorya's potential leaders have opted to work elsewhere and that Bishop John has limited human, as well as financial, resources to help him build up a new diocese.

To switch from the calving of icebergs metaphor to a horticultural model, Rorya is a tender offshoot severed from the main tree and plunged into the earth with the intention that it will establish a new life of its own. The shock of separation means that all of its energies are initially taken up in trying to establish new roots and find sustenance of its own, so it may be some time before it has the strength to achieve vigorous and visible growth above ground.

For the moment, therefore, Rorya is concentrating on completing its partially built pro-cathedral, strengthening its parish base and nurturing its clergy in order to evangelise a wider area than is now reached. In this, and other respects, the new diocese feels like Mara did twenty-five years ago when it was abruptly cut off from its former centre in Mwanza.

The main tool being used to achieve this is Kowak Christian Training Centre, the diocesan Bible School, and it was in full swing when I visited. Its 15 students seemed both committed and ambitious and when I asked them why they were there, the collective answer was that they want to study religion and then pass on their knowledge to others – 'like the disciples did with Jesus'. There was a sprinkling of women amongst them and they all assured me that they want to be pastors. There are no ordained women in either Rorya or Tarime at present (and only one in Mara) but Bishop John stressed that he has no objection to the idea.

"After all," he told me, "I was taught much of my theology by women." This referred to his period at theological college in Uganda where most of the teachers were women, and where he saw women doing ordinary parish jobs as well.

The bishop and his depleted staff are fully engaged with the building of new churches and in running the Bible School. Both of these activities are essential for the establishment of a viable presence in Rorya, but neither yet reaches out into the community, other than in a purely evangelistic way. When I asked about projects of the sort I had seen in Mara, there was nothing tangible for me to visit. Nor was there any active project designed to generate income and so fund other initiatives aimed at health, education, development, and so on.

We walked round the abandoned site of the once thriving 'Kobrix' project which used to make superior quality bricks that were sought after over the whole of

Mara Region. It was started in 1980, in pre-Mara days, when what is now Rorya was still under the umbrella of the Diocese of Victoria Nyanza. The money came from EZE, a Germany-based church organisation dedicated to the promotion and strengthening of self-reliance, and was allocated via the Christian Council of Tanzania, CCT. It was a well-chosen venture for an area rich in the raw materials needed and with an almost limitless potential demand for the end product.

All that remains of the project is a number of derelict buildings, and scattered piles of crumbling bricks. The project collapsed in 1997 (under Mara's watch) and whilst I could not discover why, there are no current plans to revive it, despite an increased demand for good bricks as Tanzania continues to develop and an emerging middle class has the disposable income with which to buy superior building materials. New buildings spring up throughout the region on almost a daily basis.

The only other project mentioned in Rorya was a plan to cultivate forty acres of land and market the maize produced. In a good year this could produce six hundred sacks of maize and £20,000 worth of income, set against a relatively small outlay for seeds and labour. Only eight acres had been cultivated so far, however, and the difficulty of paying for tractor hire was cited as the reason.

Rorya is not without ideas for development, however. Bishop John showed me an ambitious five-year plan which is all embracing and imaginative. It was carried out by an external facilitator working with a core planning team, the bishop, and parish representatives.

Included in the plan's aims is the desire to be 'a missional church, reaching out beyond ourselves (both at home and overseas) with acts of loving service and proclamation that radiate our commitment to Jesus.'

As this was just what I was looking for, I read the plan with interest. After mention of the need to develop leaders and raise the profile of the new diocese, it talks about the creation of numerous programmes, dealing with such issues as Development Relief, Children with Disability, Poverty Empowerment, Small Scale Business Training for Young People, Micro-Credit, HIV/AIDS, Community Mobilisation Against Environmental Degradation, Hunger, Community Mobilisation Against Child Labour, and a Children's Hospital. In addition to this formidable list of aspirations, Bishop John hopes to build a school complex on the abandoned Kobrix site, once ownership has been established and when Howard University in the USA agrees to fund its construction.

But with only two years to run when I visited in 2013, the plan was still just that – a plan. No similar projects have been carried over from Mara, no new ones have yet been initiated, and no funds are available with which to do so. Only the proposed school complex would generate money and so help fund other initiatives, and it was not in the five-year plan. If Howard University does give Rorya the go-ahead, however, it would still be at least two years before any income was generated and even then my own experience at Issenye suggests that it takes many years for a new school to have any surplus cash.

The only other sources of income derive from parish giving and from Rorya's link with Wakefield Diocese. The one church service I witnessed in Rorya did not bode well for the former. It was in the Cathedral and was led by a female evangelist who preached tellingly on the ways in which we all hear God's word and then largely ignore it. There was a small but excellent choir of eight girls and four boys whose voices resonated beautifully round the half-built church. The collection then followed but there was little cash handed over. Instead, there was an assortment of produce, a bundle of firewood, a sisal rope, a large pawpaw, three eggs, a box of matches and a toilet roll. These were then auctioned off at inflated but still modest prices to those of us who had money in our pockets.

As for the link with Wakefield, only thirteen of Rorya's thirty-five parishes have such a link. (Tarime has even fewer with ten links out of its twenty-seven parishes, whilst Mara has forty-nine links for its sevent-one parishes.) At the point of separation from Mara the General Fund (un-earmarked money to be used at the bishop's discretion) was split three ways, but on a proportional basis, meaning that Rorya gets one quarter of such money rather than the third that was hoped for.

Tarime was separated from Mara at the same time as Rorya, but to pick up the horticultural metaphor with which we started, the process was more like that of 'layering' than that of taking a cutting. A healthy branch was laid down on the ground and allowed to develop its own extensive root system before being severed from the main tree.

That healthy branch was Mogabiri, formerly the shining jewel in Mara's crown, and now Tarime's. The well established infrastructure, qualified and committed personnel, and existing outreach projects associated with and based at Mogabiri will be the focus of our next chapter, but their presence appears to have given the new Diocese of Tarime a flying start in contrast to its neighbour's more faltering steps.

Few things demonstrate the difference between the inheritance of the two offshoot dioceses than the transport available to each. Rorya's ancient Mitsubishi Pajero had joints and ligaments that no longer functioned as easily as they used to – a condition with which I readily empathised as it wheezed and groaned in protest on Rorya's unpaved roads. Any change in direction or level provoked a weary protest and no journey was ever guaranteed to finish as, or where, planned, despite the crucifix dangling from the windscreen. As far as I could see, it was the only vehicle other than the odd bicycle that was available to the bishop and his staff. When I reached Tarime, however, there was a row of smart four-by-fours parked outside the cathedral, and even more when I reached Mogabiri, where I was to stay. They all appeared to be in good condition and on none of the lengthy journeys I took in them was I made to feel uneasy

Bishop Mwita Akiri was lecturing (and no doubt fund raising) in Canada when I visited, but he had generously thrown open his diocese to me and I was warmly welcomed. Here, again, the emphasis is on parish development. Only 8 of its 27 parishes actually have a church building. In the remaining 19, congregations worship under trees, in makeshift shelters, or in schools, so the emphasis is on church and vicarage building.

There was no sense, however, that they were waiting for money to come pouring in from outside to fund this exercise. I was told that parishioners are being encouraged to give more realistically, and I heard echoes of the various stewardship campaigns we have all experienced in Britain over the years. They were thinking big, too. Alongside the programme of church buildings, each parish was to get a purpose-built vicarage, all constructed to the same design and big enough to accommodate any size of clerical family. I was whizzed round several of these in various stages of readiness and was encouraged by the general sense of optimism that prevailed, and by the 'can do' spirit that pervaded diocesan staff.

Mara's two offshoots have got off to very different starts and it will, perhaps, be another 25 years before judgements can be made about the success of the split from the mother diocese.

Last remnants of Kobrix project, Kowak

New vicarage under construction, Tarime

Chapter 14
Mogabiri

The road to Mogabiri rises sharply from Tarime town. In February 2013, it was being given a tarmac surface for the first time. For thousands of people this will be a welcome improvement from the original steep track, dusty when dry but deeply rutted and treacherously muddy when wet, which previously challenged every visitor. The climb was always worth the effort, though, as to reach the highlands of Mara Region is to enter another world. The higher elevation creates a cooler climate and this, combined with fertile soil, provides an agricultural haven for bananas, coffee, cassava, corn, and other crops. Lush vegetation replaces scattered scrub, with swathes of densely planted banana trees shading the rich, red earth and playing host to a variety of brightly coloured tropical birds including the coucal, popularly known as the water bottle bird which, though rarely seen, projects its deeply echoing call from tree to tree.

    The Diocese of Tarime's Mogabiri Farm Extension Centre (MFEC) lies at the end of a shady track off the main road. It is enclosed by a business like fence and backs on to the Great Rift Valley's beetling escarpment. Inside are a number of specimen trees which, as at Buhemba, bear plaques to record the presence of dignitaries invited to plant a tree. They provide an interesting record of church and government visitors from around Tanzania and the world come to see the work that goes on here.

What they see is impressive. Just inside the gate there is a collection of well-constructed guest chalets, then other buildings come into view including a church, office buildings, a dining hall, lecture rooms, and a series of low-tech agricultural structures housing cows, goats, chickens and ducks. In between them are small demonstration plots of various crops, shaded by avocado, pawpaw and banana trees.

Unlike Buhemba with its extensive thousand acres, Mogabiri's footprint is tightly constricted within a well-defined space which can be walked round in twenty minutes. All its efforts are devoted to improving the farming practices of local smallholder farmers and increasing their income through farming, conservation and the increase of agricultural and livestock production.

Mogabiri also aims to create greater awareness through education and training of extension workers, farmers and farm motivators, so the emphasis, yet again, is on education, and large numbers of local people have passed through its doors. They receive formal lessons, using modern technology with laptops, CDs, memory sticks, data projectors and screens in well furnished classrooms lit by mains electricity from the national grid, but with a powerful generator as back-up.

Following lectures they can step outside and see well ordered strips of land planted with crops that demonstrate new seed varieties, improved cultivation techniques, and modern but environmentally sound pest control. What they have seen as a Powerpoint™

presentation comes to life in ways that relate to their daily activities. Soil, seeds and plants replace chalk, talk and technicolour images. The carefully structured programme teaches crop planning and management, effective use of available resources in soil and water conservation, waste management, establishment and care of multipurpose trees, the use of agrochemicals, the practice of crop rotation, and the use of organic manure, compost and mixed cropping. The emphasis throughout is on sustainable livelihoods.

I was by now familiar with the rough hewn timber shelters used to keep cattle and goats in for zero grazing techniques, but there is an extra twist at Mogabiri as the copious waste products are used to create bio-gas with a system similar to that recently installed at Issenye. It was undergoing repairs during this latest visit, but the kitchen stoves used to cook food for the staff and students are normally fuelled in this way. Bee-keeping and poultry rearing are also on the centre's syllabus, as is money management, with a special micro-finance for women built into the course.

One innovative technology they are pioneering at Mogabiri is known as *sukuma/vuta* (push/pull) that uses selective intercropping to repel unwanted pests from food crops. The 'push/pull' strategy intercrops cereal crops with an insect repellent plant in the middle and an insect attracting plant round the edges. For example, maize can be intercropped with Desmodium, which 'pushes' pests such as the maize stem borer away from the crop, and bordered by Napier grass, which 'pulls' them so that they lay their eggs in the grass, where they do no harm, instead of in the maize, where they do. Napier grass also produces a gummy substance that traps freshly hatched stem borers so that only a few survive to adulthood. Bad news for stem borers but great for smallholder farmers and their families.

This way of dealing with pests is effective and cheap and, crucially, does not require the use of expensive and harmful insecticides or pesticides. Since its development in Kenya in 1997, the technique is claimed to have helped nearly 40,000 farmers in East Africa. According to the International Centre of Insect Physiology and Ecology in Nairobi, maize yields have increased by up to 3.5 tonnes per hectare in some areas, helping to bring 300,000 people out of hunger and poverty.

Without the expertise concentrated at Mogabiri, local farmers would have no access to any of these new technologies and would be destined to follow on in the footsteps of their parents, but with diminishing resources due to increases in population and consequent division of plots available for each family to cultivate.

I was taken to meet Michael, who was first approached by the staff at Mogabiri in 1998. He had enthusiastically adopted their advice and copied the techniques he was shown until now, fifteen years later, his life has been transformed. From being a subsistence farmer barely able to feed his family, he now has a thriving smallholding which provides him and his family with most of their daily needs and enough additional income to educate and clothe his children. After building his zero grazing unit and planting the first crop of feedstuff to supply it he was given a cow. Under the Mogabiri contract he gave away the first calf it produced to a neighbour, kept the second, and returned the third to MFEC. Everybody wins! He showed me the well dug close to his compound and then proudly posed for photographs in front of the new house he is building which will provide modern accommodation for his growing family.

Back at the centre I noticed one of the MFEC team's wives working in her small garden and went to greet her. Her plot was, unsurprisingly, super-productive and bursting with vegetables of every kind. The unusual feature, however, was a small raised bed which is not very Tanzanian, although I had seen one previously in Musoma at the house of Rehema, an AIDS victim. The walls were made of woven sticks and in the centre there was a raised funnel, leading down into the soil. I asked what it was for and she showed me, pouring liquid manure into it which she had made from farmyard waste.

"My husband told me about his way of getting a lot of vegetables from a very small area, and I decided to do it myself," she said.

Then we went to see Penina, a widow without local family support but a young son to raise on her own. She, too, had built a zero grazing unit for her cow of which she was extraordinarily proud, and had revolutionised her smallholding by planting different crops and using new techniques. She told me how much her life had improved, both in terms of better nutrition for her family and useful income from the sale of milk and produce.

"Look at my new house," she said. It was a tiny affair in reality, but built of solid brick and in stark contrast to the mud hut standing next to it which had previously been her home.

"And my son goes to school now," she continued. "Before, I could not afford to buy him shoes or exercise books, but now he will have an education and live a better life."

'Life in all its abundance' is the promise of the Gospel. At Mogabiri, they are delivering it.

Raised bed, Mogabiri

Zero grazing, Mogabiri

Chapter 15
All that glisters

Mogabiri sits perched on the rim of the Great Rift Valley which extends almost four thousand miles from Lebanon and the Red Sea in the north to Mozambique in the south. When it reaches Tanzania it divides into two, with Lake Victoria lodged between the two branches. It was formed, we are told, by unimaginable forces at work beneath the earth's surface where tectonic plates slowly grind against each other to tear the planet's land masses apart. Looking out from Mogabiri you can see the far wall of the valley, some miles away and just make out the thatched hut settlements sitting on its floor, as though seen from an aeroplane.

There had been overnight rain, with thunder and lightning to break the *kiangazi*, or dry season, and now there was an early mist here in the lush vegetation of Tarime's highlands. Tight-packed hands of bananas were ripening above my head – both the sweet ones we know in Britain and the large savoury plantains known as *matoke* that make such an acceptable alternative to potatoes and are the staple diet in many regions of Tanzania. Avocado and mango trees were dripping moisture onto the red earth, and everyone was grumbling about how cold it was. To this traveller from snowbound Britain it felt like a pleasant June day, with layered winter clothing a distant memory.

We set off on a journey to the floor of the valley, and the previous night's rain made it an interesting experience. The Toyota Landcruiser slid crabwise along the road, with pedestrians and cyclists prudently stepping out of the way at our approach. The road dropped down, down, winding through deeply forested areas then small and large plantings of *matoke*, coffee, cassava, beans, maize and millet. Small roadside stalls offered samples of produce to passers-by, and bicycles were loaded up with impossibly large bunches of bright green bananas, destined for the market in Tarime town. The weight of the bananas is such that on these uphill sections the bikes have to be pushed, but when they reach the top of the valley and head downhill again towards Tarime town, the momentum achieved will far exceed the capacity of the brakes to stop or even slow down the rider. If forced to halt, he has to dismount at speed and haul on the handlebars as if reining in a team of runaway horses, every muscle straining to avoid disaster. Inevitably, there are spillages, and everyone rushes to help the stricken rider. Cars stop to give him time to collect his precious load and resume his journey. Pedestrians right his machine and help him to stack it up again. Each load of three huge bunches can fetch up to £14 at the market, a generous week's income for a family.

We reached the valley floor, and now the sun had dispelled all trace of moisture, except that which we created with our own perspiration. The vegetation had thinned out and we drove along a dusty, rock-strewn road that crossed open savannah punctuated by the spiky leaves of sisal plants marking out areas that had been cultivated and which were now waiting for the rains to take hold for the next crop to be planted. We were in Kuria tribal country and the homesteads were tightly fenced in with long, vertical poles surrounding groups of four to six huts, depending on the size and wealth of the extended family living within. Such defensive measures are needed in this area which is currently troubled by war.

"Who is the enemy?" I asked.

"Satan," I was told. I asked if the warring is tribal in nature, as in the past Kuria and Luo people have been at odds with each other – almost always over cattle. This time, however, the fighting is between Kuria people themselves and land is at the bottom of it. In the past, Tanzania always had enough acreage to accommodate its people, but as the population grows, and families expand with more need to grow food, there inevitably comes a point where access claims are disputed and trouble breaks out. The Church's response to this issue is to accelerate its programme of parish planting and expansion.

"The unique selling point of our faith," I was told "is that we should love one another, but if there is no Christian presence in an area, this message of love and reconciliation cannot take hold." Does this explain the obsession with ecclesiastical building that grips the Church in Mara, I wonder? Faced with so many needs on which money could usefully be spent, visitors are often baffled to understand the compulsion to build a place of worship first, but perhaps there has to be a tangible focus for the people to see that the Church means business if it is to thrive. We in Britain should hardly be surprised at such a priority, moreover, when so many of our congregations find their energies being almost entirely consumed by the responsibility of maintaining an existing building.

A growing population is not the only factor in Tarime's access to land issues, though. As we looked to the right as we drove along, we could see the cliff we had recently descended, with Mogabiri lodged somewhere on its edge. To our left, in the hazy distance, was the far wall of the valley, with the majestic River Mara visible from time to time picking its leisurely way towards Lake Victoria. But now, in front of us a towering new cliff arose, blocking out the light, obstructing the view and dwarfing the huts of local residents that now seemed to be set in an alien moonscape. No grinding movement of tectonic plates had forced this barren mountain into the air, but the activity of mammon, greedy for the gold hidden beneath the feet of the impoverished people who have farmed its surface for generations past. Now, they are dispossessed, and ownership has transferred to the world's biggest gold mining company, Barrick Gold, based in Toronto. As we drew closer the colossal spoil heaps towered above us and we drove past menacing signs painted on rocks as big as a small house warning people to Keep Out. Armed guards appeared at strategic points and we glimpsed some of the gigantic machines used in the open cast workings. Barrick is tearing out the heart of Tarime in order to back up the national reserves of the developed world and decorate the wives and mistresses of the wealthy.

The physical incongruity of this large scale industrial activity with the rural simplicity that surrounds it is mirrored by a festering social disconnect that is destabilising this part of Mara Region. The people who live here know that vast wealth is being dug up from beneath their feet, but they see no benefit from it for themselves. On the contrary, they see nothing but problems. Barrick did not discover the gold – the people have always known about it and have dug it up in small quantities themselves. So-called 'artisan miners' have burrowed under their smallholdings in dangerous conditions to extract the precious ore and used it to supplement their agriculturally based incomes. Now, the land has been taken from them and the nominal payment they have been paid has not been sufficient compensation for its loss.

Many have been re-housed far from their original homes and without access to sufficient land to produce a living. Furthermore, water sources have been polluted by the dangerous chemicals used in Barrick's refinement process and people claim that they have been assailed by previously unknown illnesses as a result.

The people's reaction has been understandably hostile. One choice example I was told is too good to pass over, even should it prove to be apocryphal. Barrick has its own air strip, which is used by couriers to ferry the gold out of Mara and also by company executives too important to endure Tanzania's rudimentary road system. One young farmer, outraged at the way in which his family's life style had been turned upside down, is said to have waited on the runway and shot the pilot through the cockpit window with his bow and arrow. I want this to be true, as nothing could more accurately symbolise the clash of cultures involved.

More reliably authenticated is the incident on May 16th 2011 when five young people were shot and killed on the spot by the police at Barrick's mine. Several others were wounded, and two of them died later. They were shot because they were carrying on their traditional small scale mining activities within the area now handed over to Barrick. The Bishop of Tarime, the Rt Revd Dr Mwita Akiri, wrote an eloquent letter of reasoned protest about this incident in part of which he said:

"Put simply, with the permission of the government, Barrick came to Tarime and took away the plate of food from the table where many young unemployed people were eating. Then the investors asked those young people to go away, without looking behind. This has not happened. The unemployed young people have never gone away because neither the Mine nor the Government has given them something else to do to earn a living. So this problem is a national one: how to address youth unemployment. It is alleged (and many believe this) that each day, there seems to be some quiet arrangement between the small scale miners and the police on duty that allows those young people to go into some of the mining areas. Each day those young people come to the mine pits in hundreds if not thousands. I have seen lots of them up and down the heaped waste rock from the pits as I visit the congregations that we have in the surrounding areas."

Barrick denies any such collusion, but it is widely believed to be true, and no one doubts that illicit mining will continue, despite the well documented dangers. It has become a way of life and the hoped-for rewards are too tempting to resist. Burial in hastily dug pits and death by the gun are not the only dangers facing the people around Barrick's mine, however. In May 2009, toxic sludge from the mine seeped into the Thigithe River, a tributary of the Mara. Reports from the surrounding villages alleged that the toxic material led to the deaths of about 20 people and to fish, crops and animals dying from the contaminated water.

Barrick acknowledged that the mine had caused a spillage, but claimed it had been cleaned up and that medical experts concluded that the illnesses were 'caused by genetics, immunological or other conditions.' The Tanzanian government appears to have taken the side of the company, but an investigation sponsored by a coalition of religious groups in June 2009 assessing heavy metals around the mine found levels of cyanide higher than what is considered permissible by the World Health Organization standards.

Water samples taken from the river also found that nickel, lead and chromium levels had increased by up to 260 times since the year 2002. The report highlighted cancer, heart disease, genetic problems, respiratory complications, reproductive problems and brain damage as possible effects of exposure to toxic substances such as cyanide. The implications for areas well outside Tarime are serious as the Thigithe flows into the River Mara and eventually, Lake Victoria, shared by

Kenya, Uganda and Tanzania, but it seems that money talks and that it can also buy silence. Tarime needs its own Erin Brokovich.

"Trying to wean people away from the dream of finding gold is not easy," I was told. "Agriculture is the realistic future for our people, and education about how to improve it is our aim." We even passed a school with a message on its signboard proclaiming: "Education is better than gold." Tarime Diocese's message is that more efficient, modern farming is the answer and all the resources at its disposal emanating from Mogabiri are concentrated on helping its people focus on the achievable rather than the illusory.

Church building is also going ahead at speed. I sat in the utterly enchanting (to European eyes) temporary church at Nyorwana parish and listened to the church elders discussing how they could move forward with their plans to build a 'proper' church. Only 16 to 20 people attend on a Sunday but they plan a big *harambee*, or fund-raising celebration to get things going. Such extravagant parties are a popular element of life in Tanzania and people who can afford to do so give generously, whilst having a good time devouring copious amounts of food and drink.

"But why do you want a brick built church?" I asked.

"Nobody will take us seriously in this poor shelter," was the answer, given as though to a slow learner. They then took me along to see the small shop they have opened which sells seeds, pesticides, tools and other necessities, making them readily available for people who have no access to transport that would enable them to reach far-away Tarime town.

The dream of unimaginable wealth that has so seduced people in this part of Mara is proving difficult to dispel. Before Barrick came, digging for gold was there as a side-line for many families, who saw it in much the same way as when we buy the occasional lottery ticket in the hope that, one day, the jackpot might drop into our laps. Now that tickets are no longer on sale in Mara, attention is focussed on the well documented and guaranteed jackpot that is air-lifted out of their villages day by day. The Church's twin aim of challenging the unfairness of what is going on and at the same time offering realistic alternatives to an improved life style ticks all the boxes of Gospel-driven outreach.

No entry – Gold mine ahead

Parish seed shop, Nyorwana

Chapter 16
Water for Life

Water is essential to life, and the good news is that there's plenty of it. The bad news is that there are increasing numbers of us, and that our appetite for water grows year by year. The UK Environment Agency reports that each Londoner uses an average of 160 litres (36 gallons) of water a day. In African terms, that would involve 53 trips to the spring each day in order to satisfy the needs of the fairly average six person household

In practice, this could take more hours than there are in the day, but African people are less wasteful with water and everything else than we are. In the absence of reservoirs, piped water supplies, filtration plants and all the paraphernalia of a developed society, most people in Mara have to find ways of fetching water from where it is – almost always lower down than where it is needed despite Jack and Jill's alleged ascent of a hill– and bringing it to where it can be used. For many, that means a daily trudge to a potentially polluted water source to provide the family needs of drinking water, cooking, cleaning and washing. It also means exposure to a host of water-borne diseases such as diarrhoea, typhoid, shistosomiasis and cholera. According to the charity Water Aid, 20,000 Tanzanian children die before the age of five each year due to diarrhoeal diseases alone.

The main reason for such a horrifying statistic is that most families do not have access to clean water for drinking, cooking or washing. What they have is something that looks like a village pond, with a spring rising up in the corner. Such wells are usually managed very effectively. The first pool is where the water bubbles up from its underground source. This is where you go to fetch water, and there are three rules for those who use it. Firstly, you are not allowed to approach the water before removing your shoes. Secondly, you don't dip your bucket into the water, but use a clean jug to scoop it up. And thirdly, you do no washing in this pool. These three measures are enforced by a paid guardian, who has the authority to confiscate the water carrying buckets of any offender. After a period of time they can be bought back, and the fine imposed provides the guardian with a compelling work ethic as it is also his sole source of income.

As the water continues to flow from its source, there comes a point at which it overflows into a second pool, screened from the first by vegetation. Here, people can wash themselves, and times are strictly regulated so that men and women bathe at different periods in the day. They arrive with soap and sometimes a towel, though the hot sun may do the drying all on its own. The overflow from this pool goes into a third area where laundry takes place, and the overflow from that is directed into people's *shambas* for irrigation. Neighbouring *shambas* take turns, with channels being blocked off and re-opened in rotation.

It is a perfectly good system and, when working well, it is difficult to fault. Unfortunately, being operated by fallible human beings it can all too easily go wrong.

The chances of contamination are too many at each point of the process for it to be satisfactory. Animal and human waste finds its way into the system and vigorous but microscopic and therefore invisible wild life in surface water produces its own catalogue of dangerous conditions.

The prospect of piped and filtered water coming from reservoirs and treatment plants to every household is a distant dream for most people in Mara, but there are alternatives to the traditional trek to a spring. A great deal of rain can fall in half an hour in these latitudes and schemes to harvest it are gaining in popularity. Any roof, even one of thatch, can be used as the catchment area, then all that is needed is guttering, which can be improvised, and a holding vessel. The simplest form of this is a discarded oil drum, but ideally a more permanent and capacious receptacle is needed in the form of a concrete tank – either below ground or above it. These can be modest in size, such as those installed by the GoMAD organisation for domestic use, or more ambitious such as those at Issenye, catering for larger numbers. The water still has to be looked after and protected from contamination, but the risks are much reduced and the time-wasting chore of repeated trips to a distant spring is avoided – at least during the rainy season and for as long as the supply holds out. Where the water-table and the geology allows, the sinking of a well is a more reliable system, though that, too, may dry up from time to time.

The 'Water for Life' (WFL) scheme was set up in 2008 to mark the twentieth anniversary of the Wakefield

Mara Link. Its aim is to provide clean water, health education and skills training in twenty-four rural communities over a period of five years. It addresses water issues in a holistic way by bringing together sustainable water solutions, health education, and water management skills to selected communities which agree to co-operate in the work of creating new systems.

A team of five people in Wakefield raised £15,000 in the first two years to get things going and make assessments of what was possible. They then set a target of £2,000 for each of the twenty-four selected communities, split between cost of materials, local labour payments, health education training, supervision and oversight. This meant an ambitious overall target of £63,000 for the whole of the projected five years of the scheme. When I visited in 2013, there was still £8,000 in the kitty thanks to the vigorous efforts of the Wakefield team, supported by sponsored walks and other enterprises undertaken by people inspired by the project's aims. In Mara, Jonas Lukule, Grace Enock and water technician Max Rugembe form a 'water committee' which organises village surveys to identify the right places to work, then conducts three day workshops which cover health, hygiene, malaria, family planning and sexually transmitted diseases. Once a project is finished it is handed over to the village elders who are expected to take responsibility for maintenance and security.

Throughout the scheme the Church co-operates with the local government and, as ever, the aim is to work co-operatively with people in the villages in order to identify and implement the right solution for each community, and to include education about health and maintenance as well as technical expertise as part of the package. In this way, it is hoped that the expertise will remain in each community long after the Church has moved on. As they are expected to make a contribution to the cost, often by means of supplying labour, it is hoped that they will feel ownership of their project and so ensure its continuity after the initial burst of enthusiasm.

The WFL pumps that I saw were effective, and the people using them were proud of what, with the Church's help, they had achieved. At Bwasi, in Mara Diocese, they had even installed two pumps – one for the exclusive use of the local primary school, thus saving its pupils the daily chore of fetching water for use at school. The depth of each well varies according to the height of the water table and the local geology. Sometimes a great deal of initial digging fails to produce water, either because huge rocks prove impossible to penetrate or because there is simply no water found at the chosen location.

Max uses traditional water-divining techniques to locate the best spot, and he is usually successful, but it is not an exact science and it is discouraging for everyone when water fails to flow. There have been other disappointments which have slowed down the hoped for progress with this ambitious programme. The reports from WFL's visitors from Wakefield and from field workers in Mara throw up a whole catalogue of setbacks and difficulties but also reveal a heartening determination to overcome them and find a way round them. The digging team hits rock? Let's use dynamite to blast a way through. The villagers aren't ready to help when they can easily get water from a nearby river? Let's teach them about the range of illnesses that are affecting their children and show them how contaminated water is what is causing them. The community isn't ready to provide the input required to sink a new well? Recruit the local school to do it instead and let them get the benefit of clean water. The soil collapses round those digging the well? Learn how to make ferro-cement rings to line the pit as it is dug. Maintenance of established wells is poor through lack of local skills? Tap in to existing skills used in other fields such as bicycle and motor car maintenance.

The way in which WFL team members in Wakefield and in Mara tackle such setbacks is inspiring, but one difficulty which continues to thwart progress is a more insidious one and it threatens the philosophy of community participation and sustainability on which the project is based. When organisations such as Barrick Gold in Tarime or VIP in Mara are ready to install pumps free of charge, WFL finds it difficult to persuade neighbouring villages that theirs is the better scheme. As one exasperated volunteer remarked in Tarime Diocese:

"They're ready enough to dig for gold, but we can't persuade them to dig for water."

Whilst 'free' sounds good, such gifts come without any community involvement in the planning or execution and with no attempt to incorporate health education and maintenance training in the communities which will benefit. They are fundamentally irresponsible and result in communities failing to assume ownership of their new asset by encouraging a 'something for nothing' approach. When something goes wrong they simply wait for 'them' to come and fix it instead of working out how to get it done.

Despite all these setbacks, WFL has ploughed on and can be proud of its results. Approximately 40,000 people now have access to clean water on their doorsteps and have learned how to keep themselves and their children safe from disease. When the project is completed it is estimated that this figure will rise to 50,000. They have also taken responsibility for their own welfare by being involved in the cost and the planning and execution of their schemes, so ensuring ownership of what they have achieved and involvement in its success.

The WFL store room in Musoma is piled high with parts for pumps and other paraphernalia which Max and his team need to complete the project, which is due for completion by the end of 2013. It has been an extraordinary effort and will undoubtedly create a demand for some form of continuation, perhaps under the direct control of Mara's three dioceses and with Wakefield more at arm's length. Its importance to the health and welfare of so many people would be difficult to over-estimate.

GoMAD volunteers build a domestic water tank

Water for life pump, Bunda

Chapter 17
Healthy living

When trying to unravel the issues that the Church in Mara addresses, health is often a factor. The Water for Life project, for example, never tackles the provision of water in isolation but links it to the importance of separating dirty water from clean, and takes care to educate people about the diseases that are caused by bad water management. A well is not simply sunk and handed over, but comes with tuition about the microscopic threats to life that accompany contamination and, most importantly, how to avoid them. Training on maintenance is given and responsibility for supervision clearly established.

Similarly, when new farming or animal husbandry projects are planned, there is also teaching about diet and nutrition to accompany the provision of seeds, the building of a goat house, or the move to zero grazing with cross-bred cattle. When new varieties of sweet potato are introduced, the strange new colour is explained in terms of the carotene which produces it and which provides a vital source of Vitamin A, enhancing the function of the immune system and even helping the reproductive system to work properly. Increased milk yield and greater agricultural output are followed up by information about access to new markets and training about how to conserve and manage improved income.

As part of the Malaria Project, mosquito nets are freely handed out, but not without a teaching about how mosquitoes behave, the time of day they pose their biggest threat, and simple ways of making the immediate domestic environment less attractive to them. Health is at the heart of the Church's concept of development and of mission.

In Mara as in Britain, poor health and poverty go hand in hand. As Tanzania is one of the world's poorest countries it is no surprise that the land is full of people living their daily lives at dangerously low levels of general health. Poor diet, limited access to medical care, contaminated water supplies, and lack of knowledge about how to avoid the illnesses that afflict them make for a precarious existence that frequently leads to serious disability and death.

Aside from illness, many Tanzanians live at dangerously low levels of health for much of their lives. Except in times of famine, when harvests fail, they do not generally go hungry and are not starving to death. Their rural life style provides the means of keeping body and soul together. They do, however, frequently suffer from malnutrition, which can range from mild to severe and which often goes unrecognised within the community itself and by outsiders. A malnourished child can be pleasingly chubby and give every appearance of being well fed which, in strictly local terms, she is. A diet which consists mainly of maize flour porridge, however, may provide all the starch and carbohydrates she needs, but leave her bereft of the protein and vitamins that go to make up a balanced diet. Whilst this condition may be invisible in the village, and that can be put right by means of education, it is also routinely misunderstood by the media in Britain with regular confusion between what is malnutrition and what is hunger. Report after report from serious organisations describing malnutrition is mistakenly illustrated in the press and on television by harrowing pictures of emaciated children gazing soulfully at the camera and apparently at the point of death. They may make for dramatic reporting, and the children thus portrayed are clearly in desperate straits and in need of immediate relief. They need the 'sticking plaster' solution of immediate help. But they are unhelpful when we later see pictures of a beaming, well covered four year old and are told that she is 'malnourished'. What she needs, rather than an emergency food package, is a change of life style that is often achievable within the community by means of education and changed behaviour.

Changing behaviour is at the heart of much of the Church's work in Mara. Rather than simply giving out both literal and metaphorical pills, there is a constant effort to help people understand the causes of the conditions that affect them, and teach them how to avoid them in the first place. Prevention is always better than cure. The Mara Diocesan AIDS-ABC programme illustrates this approach perfectly. The 'B' stands for 'Behaviour' and although testing and subsequent provision of antiretroviral drugs are freely offered, they are never simply slapped on the counter, but are always accompanied by thoughtful discussion (not fierce cajoling) about how the disease can be avoided by adopting a life style that shuns promiscuity and promotes sexual fidelity.

Whilst HIV-AIDS has a fairly evident 'Health and Education' ticket on it, agricultural development and food production are not so obviously labelled. The world's answer to food problems in Africa has often been to launch a massive appeal and ship in truckloads of food. This has happened in Mara and may happen again should disaster strike in the way it did on that occasion. But to return to our malnourished child in Mara, the Church's way of helping her is through the work of the ICDP, DDP, BRAC and MFEC programmes described earlier. These initiatives link practical help with new ways of rearing stock and growing food to fresh insights into food values, nutrition and safe storage.

We have already looked at the community rehabilitation work of CBR and now we turn to Isseco Health Centre, started by Maureen Jones and which now operates under the joint direction of Issenye High School and Mara Diocese Health Department. It began with word leaking out that there was a nurse midwife at the newly opened school and people from the surrounding community began to appear for help. News spread about the effective treatment they received and a growing demand arose from an ever widening catchment area in the absence of any such help in this remote location at the edge of the Serengeti. Mobile clinics were established in distant locations and the work load increased until it became clear that some central facility would be needed to meet the demand. At the same time, teachers and students at the school needed treatment for minor ailments and the idea of a health facility catering for the school and the community took shape.

Things really took off when a child born with a severe form of talipes, or club foot, was brought to the school by a newly recruited teacher. Despite the fact that he was an educated man with a scientific background, he had never been made aware that his son could be treated, and the family expected that this child would be reliant on others for the rest of his life. When Jonah came to Issenye he was unable to walk more than three strides without falling down and could not stand up alone. He was a big boy for his age and, unusually for a Tanzanian child, he was overweight because of his enforced inactivity. He was a pleasant, happy child who would sit on the ground whilst other children played all around him.

It was clear that he needed surgery, and this was carried out by a surgeon in Arusha. The operation went ahead smoothly, and Jonah emerged from the hospital with his legs in plaster casts which totally immobilised him. Once home, Maureen changed the casts weekly – a process that was to continue for more than three months. Each time, she massaged his feet to encourage the straightening process. As plaster is messy stuff, all this took place on our veranda, often in full view of an interested audience from school and village. When the final cast came off, Jonah's feet needed more massage and manipulation, and he was able to don smart new boots, the first footwear he had ever been able to use and a great status symbol. In less than a week he was happily playing football alongside his companions.

People had believed, up till then, that nothing could be done about talipes. It was considered to be '*Kazi ya Mungu*' (The Work of God) and therefore unalterable. The Church in Mara, however takes the view that God gives doctors and nurses the skills to correct deformities and that exercising those skills is also '*Kazi ya Mungu*'. The effect on the surrounding community of seeing Jonah racing about the school campus with straightened feet was to bring people round to this point of view. Child after child was carried to the school, with pleas for help to 'make him like Jonah'. This meant that from then on all children affected by talipes in that area could be treated at an early stage by simple manipulation, and thus avoid surgery. Parents themselves were taught how to continue the treatment, as is done routinely in Britain, and now also at the CBR clinic in Musoma.

In Britain, the word 'dispensary' summons up the image of a window in the hospital where you collect the medicines prescribed by a doctor, but Issenye's dispensary did far more than that from the very beginning. It very rapidly developed into a full-blown health centre delivering immunisation and maternity services.

Twenty years after Jonah's arrival I walked round with Elyas, the doctor in charge who, along with his two nurse midwives and one cleaner, manages to offer a 24 hour service to the 600 strong school community and to families from many miles around. There are now three wards, along with a small laboratory, examination room and storage facilities. Electric lighting comes from the school generator each evening, and from solar panels in the remaining hours of darkness. A large water tank collects rainwater from the roof, which is then pumped up to a header tank allowing it to fall by gravity to a stainless steel sink for hand washing. The tap is a push-button type, which cannot be left running. There is also an outside tap which supplies water from the school's well.

    The walls were painted and clean, the floor freshly swept and a busy hum of activity met me as I went in, to be joined by Esther, a former Issenye student who is now head nurse midwife at the dispensary. We exchanged greetings and I watched as she and Elyas busied themselves with the queue of smiling mothers and two fathers gathered in front of the building waiting to have their babies weighed at the morning's Mother and Child (MCH) clinic. The process provoked a good deal of hilarity as each child was suspended from a beam in a small harness and his weight carefully recorded in a register, with a copy for each mother. Some took to their sudden weightlessness with ease, swinging round and gazing at the world round-eyed but without distress. Others set up a howl of protest as soon as they were parted from their mother's back, only to subside when released from the strange contraption.

    The MCH Clinic is so popular and so well used that Elyas now plans to build a separate building to house it and so establish a degree of separation between these healthy children and the sick people either admitted to a ward or waiting to see the doctor. A plan has been drawn up and, reflecting the healthy finances of the school these days, it has agreed to contribute £2,400 towards the total estimated cost of £7,000.

On alternate days there is a clinic just for children, and this is when the health centre carries out its immunisation programme. Such work is normally done by government dispensaries, but at Issenye the authorities took the unusual step of appointing Isseco Health Centre as the designated delivery point. This happened early on after a visit by the Regional Director of Health who was visibly impressed by the amenities, which were in embarrassing contrast to the government's own local facility.

There is now a gas-powered fridge at the dispensary, installed by the government to store the vaccines for the very comprehensive range of immunisation delivered there. Without any Tanzanian version of Dr Andrew Wakefield to arouse unwarranted alarm about MMR, Tanzanian parents have sensibly taken everything on offer and at Issenye their children are immunised against measles, tuberculosis, polio, pneumonia, diarrhoea, diphtheria, tetanus, and hepatitis. In addition to this impressive range of protection, they are shielded from malaria whilst still in the womb by the SP tablets given to their mothers during pregnancy.

Yet again, this facility demonstrates the way in which the Church in Mara has responded to a need within the community and has done so in a way that is self sustaining. Although the immunisation and child care treatment are free, maternity and other services are chargeable, and the health centre is run as a business, balancing its books at the end of each year. It is true that, for capital development, it has relied on outside funding from Wakefield (Golcar and Battyeford in particular) and that such help will still be needed during its development stage. The proposed new MCH facility is a case in point. When it is built, Isseco Health Centre should be able to stand on its own two feet and provide a model for future initiatives throughout Mara.

But there is a limit to how far such a village resource can and, indeed, should be developed. More serious conditions cannot be treated at Issenye and the more it begins to feel like a hospital, the greater is the risk of something going wrong. There are properly equipped and staffed hospitals at Bunda and Mugumu, both one and a half hours away on a good day, and Musoma, two and a half.

Mothers queuing, Isseco Health Centre

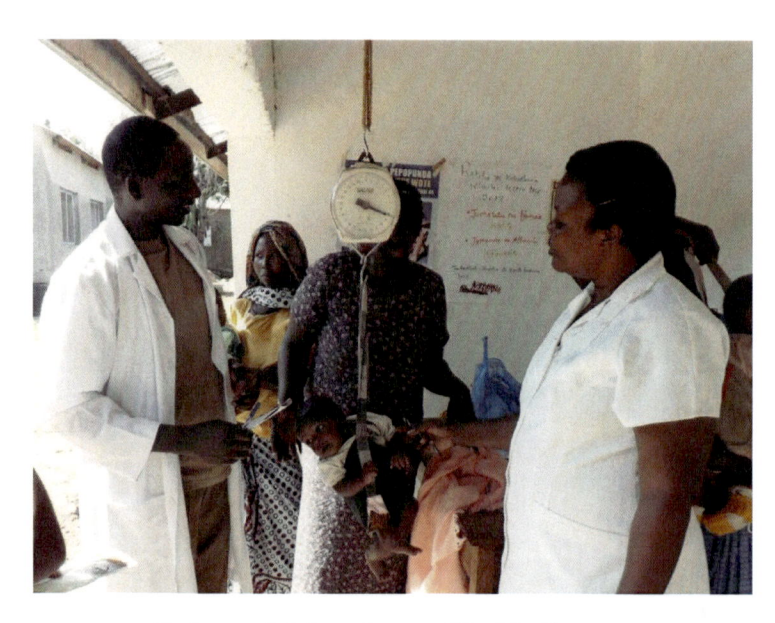

Baby weighing, Isseco Health Centre

Chapter 18
Finale

On my last day in Mara in 2013 I was sitting outside the Afrilux early in the morning, waiting for a taxi to take me to Musoma's air strip. From there I was to take a half hour flight in a small plane to Mwanza, on the first leg of the journey home. In front of the Afrilux there is a neatly tiled area, inlaid with different colours to represent a map of Africa. The map is distorted, making Africa look fatter than it is. Fatter, certainly, than the Petersen Projection now favoured by cartographers, which shows it as a lean and elongated continent.

The young man sweeping leaves from its surface in preparation for the daily wash, however, was pure Petersen – tall and skinny to the point of emaciation. He was wielding a locally made besom, carefully assembling a deposit of leaves into a tidy pile which he moved steadily southwards from Egypt and Sudan, towards the equator. When he reached northern Kenya, however, the fickle morning breeze changed direction and surged northwards, undoing his efforts and causing him to pause.

He stoically accepted the situation and began to sweep northwards, like a human weathercock, reacting to instant change. He reached Egypt for a second time and was about to sweep across the Mediterranean when, once again, the wind shifted southwards and he was obliged to face about and aim for the distant Cape of Good Hope.

My taxi arrived at this point and as I was driven to the air strip I pondered the living metaphor I had just witnessed.

The winds of change have not always blown kindly across Africa. So many projects, dreams, plans and targets, whether devised by governments, aid agencies, or individuals, are affected by changes beyond the control of the planner. Rains fail, so harvests are meagre; donors change priorities, so projects are left stranded; corrupt officials divert funds, so roads are not maintained; new diseases such as AIDS spring to life and monopolise health resources; tribal or religious animosities put machetes and Kalashnikovs into young men's hands instead of ploughshares, so fields go untended and food crops are not planted.

And so progress is blighted and development takes one step backwards for every two forwards. For all I know, the leaves in front of the Afrilux were still swirling around the equator as I boarded my plane, and the young man's efforts, whilst taking up all his time and his energy, were achieving little. Many of the thoughtful people I talked with on this journey spoke with deep frustration about the way in which countries like India and China are forging ahead whilst they feel themselves to be permanently condemned to poverty.

I urge them to think positively and look at those things they *have* achieved. In the thirty years that I have known Tanzania, the country has been transformed. It may be a surprising example to choose, but I was moved by the sight of a row of children's bicycles in front of a Musoma shop, still in their manufacturer's wrappings.

I had already marvelled at the solar panels, generators, motor cycles, polytanks, bottled water, mobile phones, extending ladders and internet cafes – none of which existed in the austere 1980s. But it was the sight of these frivolous things, children's toys, which now stirred me. Time for leisure is surely one of the hallmarks of development, and although most of Musoma's inhabitants would still be unable to buy those bicycles, shopkeepers do not stock things for which there is no market. Of course, Musoma still has people in rags with little opportunity for leisure in their daily struggle for survival and who go to bed hungry, but the gap between rich and poor in Tanzania is smaller than in their envied rivals, China and India. An educated middle class is emerging, and things are getting better. And who knows – perhaps Tanzania's slower, more organic growth may prove in the end to be longer lasting than those based on supplying the west with cheap fridges.

The Anglican Church is playing a significant part in that growth with its Gospel-driven determination to offer unconditional service not only to the communities in which it is placed, but also to those on which it has set its sights.

I remember the notice on the wall of Buhemba's manager - *'We think that what we are doing is just a drop in the ocean, but oceans would be less because of that missing drop.'* I remember the almost daily encounters wherever I go in Mara with former Issenye students now making their way in the world; the hundreds of small scale farmers who have been able to educate their children after being shown how to be more efficient and productive; the families living with AIDS who have been given new purpose in life; the thousands of villagers who now have access to safe, clean water on their doorstep and who are thus given a better chance of avoiding a galaxy of life-changing illnesses, and the many, many more thousands of individuals whose lives have been ameliorated and transformed by the activities I have been privileged to witness during my time in Mara. I think of all these things, and I want to cheer.

My last service in Mara was at St John's Cathedral, Musoma, on Palm Sunday. There was no need to import tiny dried palm leaf crosses from the Holy Land, as parishioners simply tore bright green living fronds off the palms surrounding the cathedral. We paraded round the outside of the cathedral, then trooped past all the diocesan offices in a noisy procession, waving our palm leaves in the air and commemorating the triumphal march of Jesus into Jerusalem. The sermon which followed went something like this: 'Jesus came, not to be fêted like a king, as he was on that first Palm Sunday but to offer, through his ministry as a *servant* king, the perfect example of how we should live together. We must, therefore, learn to love each other and pray for each other - whoever we are. And the prayer that comes out of this should lead us into seeking ways of serving each other, at whatever cost.' Anyone who has attended Church in Africa will appreciate that this is a severely condensed version, but who could not say 'Amen' to its core message?

I left Mara on this most recent visit full of exhilarating thoughts. I am convinced that the Church there is living the Gospel, 'using words if necessary' but frequently dispensing with them altogether in its determination to address the inequalities and difficulties faced by the people living in the communities it serves. At the same time, the Church is growing, both in terms of numbers joining its activities and as a significant player in the life of the nation.

Does this mean that people in Mara flock to church simply because of the 'deeds' they see being enacted in its name? Not so. Each of Mara's three dioceses takes the training and strengthening of its clergy and evangelists seriously, and not simply as an arm of social services to the community. The Gospel is preached and lives are changed. The Bible Schools at Buhemba and Kowak train men and women to lead people to Jesus and spread the message of Christian love within the communities from which they have come and to which they will return. They model themselves on St Paul and his companions, taking the Gospel into virgin territory and claiming it for Christ, rather than exhorting them to return to something that they, or their parents, used to do.

But it is difficult to imagine anyone in Mara declaring that they started going to church because they now believed in God. They almost certainly did that anyway, in one form or another. And so the decision is based on other factors. What do they see when they look at the Church? It seems to me that they see an organisation actively engaging with the community. It is clear that the Church there has a markedly different image from that which it has in Britain, and this may be explained at least partly by its outreach into the community and its ubiquitous presence there alongside government and other agencies as part of their everyday lives.

But how can we in Britain learn from this if we, too, want to grow our Church and serve our communities because, like them, that is what we believe our faith obliges us to do? We can't turn the clock back and reclaim our schools, almshouses and hospitals. They may still have names like St James's and St Mary's which speak to their origins, but for the most part they are now firmly under secular control and subject to no more than peripheral influence from the Church. And we can't set up fish farms in Flockton or goat sheds in Golcar. Our society is so developed that there is less elbow room for manoeuvre than in Mara where the Church sees yawning gaps in provision and, provided it can raise the resources in terms of cash and personnel, it can wade in and get things done.

But that does not mean that there is no elbow room at all. Can we, perhaps, learn from Mara that it may be more effective to preach the Gospel by delivering it first, and then seeing what happens, rather than relying on words? Instead of saying 'come back to church', can we simply say 'see what the Church is doing' and wait for people to want to be part of it? The Church in Mara does not very often talk about how to fill the church building. What it does talk about is problem solving. The conversation goes like this.

"People are suffering from AIDS (or hunger, malaria, poverty, dirty water, ignorance…....) so what can we as Christians do about it? Let us identify the problem, assemble some expertise, formulate a solution, calculate the cost, find what partners we can work alongside, get the money together and set about making things better. Why? Because Jesus came to bring abundant life and it's up to us, as the Body of Christ, to deliver it. Is it just for our congregations? No! If Jesus had restricted his ministry to those who already believed in him he would have had a thin time of it. So let's get out there and see what happens."

And what frequently does happen is that people notice what the Church is doing and want to be part of it. 'See how those Christians love each other' is extended and modified into 'See how they love us, too' and congregations grow.

"Why doesn't your Bishop open a church round here?" I was asked in one village where diocesan project workers were actively involved with a group of farmers, providing training, supervision and a small amount of seed capital to get things going. The door was wide open for church planting. Bishop Hilkiah reports that he is frequently approached by government officials urging him to open parishes in new areas, because they know that this will bring development in its wake. He is also charged with delivering government services such as the provision of antiretroviral drugs or famine relief because of the Church's unrivalled network of people on the ground. And he does not let the scale of any task daunt or deter him. He once described to me his approach to a seemingly impossible task in terms of a man trying to get through a small gap in an impenetrable thicket.

"If I can get my head through and see a way out," he said, "I feel sure that my shoulders and then the rest of me will follow, but I don't wait to find out if that is true. I just start pushing and know that if what I am trying to do is what God wants, I am bound to succeed."

Are we too often daunted by the difficulty of 'selling' Christianity in our secular society to put our trust so recklessly in God? And what, after all, is our primary Christian objective? Is it to re-stock our churches with the lost worshippers of earlier times, or is it to change our country in ways that make it conform more to Christian principles – to make the offer of 'abundant life' more widely available than it is at present?

And could it be that, in doing the latter, we might achieve the former? Could we, too, catch the fever that makes Africans want to be like St Paul and the Apostles and become convinced that the Good News is *too* good to be kept to ourselves? To do that, we must be more active, more visible and more ready to find ways of bridging the gap that now exists between church and everyday life here in Britain. We must make God less of a stranger to ourselves and to our communities. The Gospel of love and service as perfected in the life and ministry of Jesus was rarely proclaimed in the Temple. More often it was shown and acted out on a street, in a field, up a mountain, by a lake, and at the side of a well…. *as it still is in Mara*. Perhaps the principal message coming to us from Africa is simply that we should get out more.

Children's bicycles, Musoma

Solar panels, Musoma

Postscript

The first word you are likely to hear in Mara is '*karibu*'. It means 'welcome', or more literally, 'come closer'. And the very last words as you leave will almost certainly be '*karibu tena*', 'welcome again'; in other words, please come back. And you will want to.

African hospitality is legendary, and in Mara every visitor is seen as a blessing. Why wouldn't you want to go! From the smiling Bishop Hilkiah to every last villager the message is clear– please come and spend a little (or a lot) of time with us. Whether it's a two week safari taking in some of Tanzania's spectacular wildlife as well as seeing the Church in action, or a spell volunteering in one of Mara's many educational, health and social welfare projects, the door is open and you will be given every assistance to make this a most memorable experience.

As a tourist you could easily take in the Serengeti National Park, described by naturalists as one of the world's last remaining true wildernesses. Half of it is actually within Mara Diocese and there is easy access through either Ndabaka Gate, on the Mwanza road from Musoma, or Ikoma Gate, about an hour's drive from Issenye. It offers an unrivalled exposure to Africa's breathtaking scenery and magnificent wild life. You will have close encounters – unlike those countries in which binoculars are needed to see much of anything. But you will see wildlife long before you enter the park – there is no fence and the animals can't read the signs that mark its boundaries. Your vehicle may be flagged down by baboons on the tarmac road to Mwanza, and you could have to slow down for more than one zebra crossing on the way to Ikoma. The tented camps and lodges within all the parks are luxurious and up to international standards. The one closest to Issenye is called Seronera Wildlife Lodge and is an architectural masterpiece, tucked into a *kopje*, one of the Serengeti's mighty granite outcrops which lions and other predators use as lookouts across the endless plain. The Seronera and Grumeti Rivers are both within reach, and there is a designated hippo pool nearby where there are always large numbers of hippos and crocodiles to watch and photograph. Leopards and cheetahs are more elusive, but tour drivers keep in touch with each other by radio and now mobile phone, so you have a good chance of seeing a variety of wildlife.

The Serengeti's great migration is a continuous movement of 1,200,000 wildebeest and 750,000 zebra along with gazelles and other plains animals following the grass produced by seasonal rains. The wildebeest somehow synchronise their birthing to produce half a million calves within a two to three week period between February and March each year on the short grass plains of the Ngorongoro Conservation Area. As the rains there end in May the animals start moving north west, into the area around the Grumeti River, where they usually remain until late June. When they have eaten all the grass in that area they head north, arriving on the Kenyan border and crossing into the relatively small but well advertised Maasai Mara in late July or August for the remainder of the dry season. In early November with the start of the short rains they start moving south again, usually arriving back in Ngorongoro in December in plenty of time for calving again in February.

This time-table is not written in stone – it depends on rainfall patterns and subsequent growth of the grass which is the sole purpose of the migration. Every few years the route wobbles north and westwards through the populated parts of Mara Diocese, streaming through the villages and even, on one memorable occasion, through the school campus at Issenye. At these times villagers (and students) eat well, as once out of the park the animals are fair game. It's not all good news, however, as the great herds of wildebeest, eland, topi, zebra and other herbivores eat all the grass which would otherwise be available for the domesticated cows, sheep and goats of the population. Farmers then have to move their herds to other, more distant areas until the intruders have moved on to pastures new.

Other National Parks within reach are Ngorongoro Conservation Area, with its unique Crater which almost guarantees you a view of a rhino, Manyara with its tree climbing lions and the wonderful Tarangire, famous for Baobab trees and elephants. This park is relatively compact and the Tarangire River never dries up, so animals can always be found there.

No visit to Mara is complete without at least a few days wondering at nature's diversity, and there are tour firms to suit all budgets ready to create a tailor made safari. The most economic package is when you are able to fill a vehicle – normally six people – so as to share the cost. Takim's Holidays (www.takimsholidays.com) have an office in Arusha and have proved helpful and reliable for a number of years. Park fees range between $45 and $70 a day, which is steep in comparison with other countries, but this is seen as a conservation measure which helps keep the wilderness wild. It is still cheaper than a couple of hours in a London theatre and it is what helps to pay for rangers to combat the poachers who threaten to decimate the wildlife throughout Africa.

If you go to Mara as a volunteer, you will have help in acquiring the necessary visa and/or work permit as well as free accommodation and, depending on the project chosen, meals and a small allowance. The Anglican Hostel next to St John's Cathedral, Musoma offers basic accommodation, with all main facilities starting at £6 a night, or you could stay in one of the recently opened smart hotels with all mod cons for about £24.

"What's the food like in Mara?" is one question that tends to crop up frequently. Well, it's fresh! Fish straight out of Lake Victoria, beef from cattle slaughtered that morning, eggs taken from hens just around the corner, fruit and vegetables grown without harmful pesticides or artificial fertiliser. Bottled water is cheap and plentiful as are soft drinks such as Coca-Cola, Fanta and Sprite. Instant coffee from plantations up the road and tea from neighbouring Kenya, with locally brewed beers and wine from South Africa are all freely available at reasonable prices for those with money in their pockets.

If you choose to stay in the heart of Musoma town, the Afrilux Hotel makes the perfect base. On four floors, it has 23 rooms including singles, doubles and triples. All are ensuite, with bath, shower attachment, washbasin and lavatory. There is a fan, TV, air conditioner and fridge. There is usually hot water each morning, though this and other facilities are subject to the sporadic power cuts which affect all of Tanzania. There is a back-up generator. The friendly, English speaking staff change bedding and towels every day, and give the tiled floors a good mopping down. There is a bar and a dining room as well as a shaded outside patio area. Prices start at Tsh 25,000 (£10) a night, which includes a hearty breakfast. Meals are £2 to £4 each, a beer is £1 and soft drinks 40p.

There are other, more expensive and pretentious options, but they are out of town, involving either a long walk or a taxi ride to reach anywhere, whilst the Afrilux is near the town centre and close to the lake with its crowded fish markets and bustling waterfront. It is where African business men and women stay and it's the place to be. Town centres are subject to some disadvantages, and light sleepers may not relish being woken at 5am by a number of competing muezzins, though they may be entertained by Musoma's roving dog population who have taken to joining in with mournful canine salutes to the advent of dawn.

So what could you do as a volunteer? One option is to go mad! The well established 'GoMAD in Tanzania' organisation (*hannah@GoMAD.org.uk*) offers a number of different opportunities each year. 'MAD' stands for 'Make a Difference' in this context and its predominantly young volunteers do just that. Started by Graham

McClure from St John's Church, Blackheath, GoMAD now partners with Tearfund to send around 85 enthusiastic volunteers each year in teams of about 15. Most are Christians, but volunteers with different or with no religious affiliation are welcome as long as they can identify with GoMAD's objectives. The organisation's twin aims are to make a real difference to the lives of the people they work with in Mara and also to give its volunteers the opportunity to be changed by the experiences they undergo as part of one of its teams.

 I caught up with one team in the organisation's impressive self-build house overlooking Lake Victoria. There were fourteen young people, average age 19, on an eleven week project, supervised by Graham himself. They were nearing the end of their time in Mara and had achieved much, including the building of a church, three water tanks, a toilet and shower for a terminally ill person, a chicken shed and two goat sheds. They had also given three goats away, delivered health teaching lessons, transported people to hospital, run a sports club for children, taught Sunday School classes and sung in church. They had raised Tshs 33,000,000 (£13,200) between them in sponsorship money to do all this and, as I arrived, were discussing how to raise the £500 still needed to complete their work.

 We enjoyed a meal together and then they each volunteered their high spots and low spots of the day, commending all their efforts to God and offering prayers for the people of Mara whose lives they were affecting, and who were at the same time making so deep an impression on them.

GoMAD offers holidays as well as work. Some of the team were heading for Zanzibar, in a few days time and were looking forward to relaxing on its pristine beaches for a few days as reward for their exertions in Mara.

The Diocesan High School at Issenye offers a variety of volunteering opportunities. Many young people have spent periods varying between two or three weeks and six months doing a variety of jobs ranging from teaching in class to painting walls, making bricks, installing solar electricity and coaching sporting skills. They have all engaged fully with the staff and students out of hours with games, music and socialising providing stimulus for all parties. Many have found the inspiration for future career choices during their time at Issenye. The school's dispensary and health centre attracts those interested in health issues and its nursery school provides a wonderful setting for getting close to very young children and helping them in their early years learning.

Accommodation for guests is simple, but adequate, at the 'Savoy' with its bedrooms set round an enclosed courtyard, mosquito nets, loos and washing facilities, and its superb dining hall where nobody goes hungry. Issenye is sixty miles from the nearest town of any size, Musoma, so visitors get the full African experience. The Savoy is regularly used by visitors from within Tanzania so there are frequent opportunities for lively discussion and cultural interchange. You may even pick up a bit of Swahili.

If Issenye sounds a bit too rural, why not stay in Musoma itself? Population estimates suggest that some

120,000 people live there, a quarter the population of either Leeds or Sheffield, and closer to that of Huddersfield with its 146,000 people. But there all similarity ends. Musoma lies at the mouth of the Mara River as it debouches into Lake Victoria and has a fantastic but as yet totally undeveloped potential for tourism. This is small scale, easily accessible and relaxed urban Africa – unused to tourists as yet and utterly enchanting to those who want something different. Its crowded market offers every kind of tropical vegetable, fruit and grain at knock-down prices in European terms, locally produced fabrics, tools and artefacts of every kind to stare at and ponder over. The butchery stall may be hard to take for more sensitive visitors, but everything is fresh and wholesome. Whilst in Musoma and the whole of Mara you will eat nothing but natural food, uncontaminated by preservatives or additives of any kind.

There are numerous small cafés where you can get a nourishing meal of rice and beans washed down with a cup of tea or a soft drink and still get change from a pound. You can wander down to the lake side and watch the dhows bringing in their catches of *dagaa*, perch and tilapia to be piled up on the shore for distribution to market traders. Further along you may see boat builders and repairers working with hand tools to restore damaged vessels to serviceable condition. It is even possible to organise a boat trip if you are feeling adventurous, but don't expect a handy gang-plank, life belt or health and safety check. Clapped out taxis will take you to most local destinations for a pound or two and you may even risk a *boda boda* adventure on the back of one of the town's motor-cycle taxis for 40p.

Because it is not on the tourist map you will not be pestered to buy trinkets, change money or buy postcards. And because there is no white 'colonial' presence in Tanzania you will not feel the underlying resentment that can taint relationships in some corners of the former British Empire. In fact, *Tanganyika*, as it was formerly known, was never a British colony, but became a protectorate, mandated to Britain by the League of Nations after the First World War. Before that it had been a German colony, known as German East Africa. Following World War II it was designated as a United Nations trust territory under British supervision. It achieved independence peacefully and with little controversy in 1961. It remained within the Commonwealth and two years later formed a union with the Island of Zanzibar and assumed the new name of Tanzania.

All this is in marked contrast to the experiences of neighbouring Kenya which has a history of white domination marked by dispossession and violence culminating in the bitter *Mau Mau* rebellion of the 1950s. Europeans living in Tanzania are generally doctors, nurses, teachers, engineers, agriculturalists and church workers who are seen as 'there to help' rather than in it for themselves, so relationships are always good. As you walk around Musoma you will go largely unnoticed, but will always receive friendly help and advice whenever it is called for.

As everywhere, there are bad people as well as good and your skin colour identifies you out as being wealthy, even though you may not feel so. It is sensible, therefore, to take the same precautions as in any town in Britain when it comes to stowing away your wallet, passport and loose change. As for taking photographs, it is not polite to thrust your camera into people's faces without permission, which will often be granted if requested. Many Tanzanians, however, believe that tourists make money by selling their pictures to National Geographic or other western magazines. This may flatter you, but may also lead to an expectation of payment.

So what will you do in Musoma if you stay as a volunteer rather than a visitor? The Church has projects which welcome volunteer assistance within easy reach of town, such as the diocesan primary school at Nyamatare and the vocational training centre next to the cathedral. You could help out the Rehema project which supports vulnerable women and children, and also take part in the daily life of the Church. Your programme can be discussed with Mara Link Officer, Stephen Spencer, in Wakefield and the Wakefield Link Officer, Arthur Mauya, in Musoma. Their jobs have similar titles, and both involve excessively long hours, but are otherwise radically different from each other. On a recent visit to England Arthur went shopping for a motion activated security light for his house on the banks of Lake Victoria. When pressed by the assistant about exactly what he wanted it for, he told him that it was to deter the hippopotamuses climbing up from Lake Victoria and stripping his vegetable garden of cabbages. When I was last there his wife, Anna, told me that the week before they had been woken up in the night by the sound of a large bull elephant rampaging through the compound smashing down trees and crashing into houses. The army were called out and they dispatched it with a hail of bullets as a threat to life. Next day the villagers were given 24 hours to cut off what meat they could take home before the remaining carcase was destroyed. I imagine that life is a little quieter in Brighouse. Arthur's other job is Diocesan Director of Education, with oversight of Mara's Primary, Secondary and Vocational Training institutions, so he has a heavy work load, but still finds time to accommodate the needs of visitors.

"All guests are a blessing," he says, echoing the words of everyone from the Bishop onwards in the true spirit of African hospitality, which is illumined by the principle that the visitor bestows a gift on the host simply by turning up.

If you have reached so far without skipping a chapter or two, you will have sensed my own deep affection and strong admiration for Tanzania and its people. My spirits soar every time I set foot on its soil and the recollection of strong friendships and wonderful experiences stays with me long after I have returned. Like many others, I am in intermittent touch with people I met there more than 20 years ago, and Africa is buried deep within me. So will it be with you – guaranteed!

Needless to say, things must be organised before you travel, and it should be emphasised that you will be going as a short term volunteer – not a 'worker', even though what you do may feel very much like work.

Tanzania, like Britain, has strict laws about employment and immigration, and they are properly enforced. Visitors who have proudly announced that they have come 'to work' have found themselves in difficulties with the authorities and have risked embarrassing the Church.

Whatever you do, it will change you and if you don't want to be changed, don't go! The many, many numbers of those who have taken this step over the last 25 years, however, have returned to Britain with their faith refreshed, their insight into third world issues deepened, and their outlook changed. I finish with the words you will hear again and again in Mara - *Karibu!*

Tarangire National Park

Afrilux Hotel, Musoma

Lake shore, Musoma

By the same author

School for the Serengeti
The Story of Issenye
Aliquid Novum
2007

Shoulder to Shoulder
The Making of the Mara Link
Diocese of Wakefield Mara Link Committee
2008